THE ECOLOGY
OF HOUSING
DESTRUCTION

INTERNATIONAL CENTER FOR
ECONOMIC POLICY STUDIES BOOKS

The International Center for Economic Policy Studies, a nonprofit, nonpartisan institute which conducts and publishes economic research, was founded in 1977. The aim of ICEPS is to provide readable, though analytical, publications, which improve public understanding of economic problems and the market process and, where possible, suggest solutions. Its studies, which are financed with contributions from individuals, corporations and private foundations, are prepared by scholars who engage in independent research and arrive at their own conclusions about the issues they consider. Thus, while the studies reflect the areas of interest of the Directors, the Staff and the academic advisers to ICEPS, the views they present are entirely those of their authors and do not carry the endorsement of either the Directors or the sponsors of the Center.

THE ECOLOGY OF HOUSING DESTRUCTION

Economic Effects of Public Intervention in the Housing Market

PETER D. SALINS
Chairman, Department of Urban Affairs
Hunter College, City University of New York

Published by New York University Press
for the
International Center for Economic Policy Studies
1980

To Rochelle and Jessica with love

Library of Congress Cataloging in Publication Data

Salins, Peter D
   The economics of housing destruction.

   Bibliography: p.
   Includes index.
   1. Housing—New York (City)   2. Housing policy—
New York (City)   I. International Center for Economic
Policy Studies.   II. Title.   III. Title: Housing
deterioration.
HD7304.N5S28   363.5′09747′1   79-3845
ISBN 0-8147-7811-9
ISBN 0-8147-7812-7 pbk.

Manufactured in the United States of America

CONTENTS

FOREWORD

This is a scholarly book which, if read with attention, could open the door to plentiful housing for a great city that has felt itself physically cramped for more than thirty years.

New York's government has grappled so long and so unsuccessfully to improve and expand its livable residential space that its failure to do so is often viewed as a peculiar feature of the local scene, by implication unchangeable. Nothing could be further from the truth. Historically, New York has been on the cutting edge of residential innovation and production. Manhattan in particular became at once the nation's richest and most thickly populated community not by being a place that only the wealthy could inhabit with comfort, but a teeming center where people of all backgrounds and income levels could seek access to a vibrant world of risk and opportunity. This feeling still exists, but it is hard to sustain when the idea of moving to Manhattan appears to require not just a spirit of adventure but a postgraduate degree in the ways and means of doing so.

Professor Salins shows that the outer boroughs are on the way to replicating Manhattan's residential climate that invites the well-to-do and the dependent, but not those in between. The rapid expansion of affluent enclaves like Brooklyn Heights, Park Slope and Riverdale in an overall context of widening and leapfrogging "zones of destruction" is far from accidental. With the incentives for abandonment built into New York's housing policy, it is only the very well-off who have the means to cosset themselves in residential bastions like Manhattan's East Side.

How did New York get itself into this frustrating cycle? Professor Salins' methodology is well-suited to bringing out an answer that is complex yet in the end totally coherent. In an ongoing attempt to make rental housing more available to New Yorkers of moderate and low income, the city's leaders adopted a series of measures that commanded strong popular support at the time but later caused dislocation and shortage. As each policy in turn proved counterproductive, the government intervened anew to correct the undesired effect, sometimes ameliorating it but in nearly every instance triggering a new series of unintended distortions. The eventual result: a complex superstructure of cross-cutting practices and regulations that, taken together, have led to a climate marked by extreme volatility, incentives for net destruction of the housing stock, and economic polarization unmatched in any other American city.

The greatest virtue of this book is that, once the dynamic of the city's residential suicide is grasped, Professor Salins' solutions suggest themselves. A phase-out of rent regulation, cashing out the welfare housing allowance, ending two-party rental checks, and dividing rent delinquency from the rest of the landlord-tenant adjudication structure would go very far in themselves to turn the situation around. By adopting these policies, it seems clear, New York's political leaders could in fairly short order return this great city to an era of residential abundance and diversity that would benefit every citizen and enhance every other element of urban life.

At a time when other municipalities are flirting with the route New York embarked on three decades ago, publication of Peter Salins' illuminating study is especially timely. As our third book and our first on urban economics, ICEPS is proud to have sponsored a work of such clarity that, if translated into new policies, can only expand the horizons of millions of people in our home city and beyond.

Jeffrey Bell
President
International Center for Economic Policy Studies
November 1979

INTRODUCTION

Simple economics can explain much of the fiscal difficulties in which the City of New York has found itself. The "fiscal crisis" can be attributed, in large part, to changes in the technology of communications and transportation, which have led to decline in the economic base of the city and the region it serves. To the extent this is its cause, the decline is self-limiting. With change in the land prices and tax-prices associated with a central location, the trend can be expected to reverse, as it has already done in central Manhattan.

But there is more to the plight of New York than this. Though New York has prospered, historically, because of its advantages as a market, it has done so despite endemic public intervention, and the private costs of adapting to it. The most familiar instrument of such intervention is rent control, which has been in force, in one incarnation or another, since World War II. While rent control has received most of the press, however, it is but the tip of the iceberg; regulation in New York, through a motley assortment of licensing practices and buildings and land use controls, with some direct price controls added for good measure, seems pervasive. Separately, many of these controls, in direct consequence, seem innocuous, or consistent with legitimate public purpose. Together, given the full effect of administrative intervention on the market-clearing process, a different conclusion emerges. Self-serving political action and benevolent intention, interacting with administrative procedure, appear to have left New York far worse off, as a site for business and residence, than it should be.

Not only the most apparent, but the most pernicious forms of intervention occur in the market for housing. Regulation in the housing market has led to more rapid destruction of the housing stock and created more social problems than the normal processes of neighborhood decline, subject to the vagaries of the market, could ever have engendered. The problem is heightened because so much of the housing stock is renter-occupied in New York. Since tenants need not bear the full cost of failure to preserve what they have, they have weaker incentives to do so.

These phenomena are examined by Professor Peter Salins in the *Ecology of Housing Destruction*. Although there are many dimensions to Salins' argument, its thrust is that intervention has contributed to the devastation of vast areas of the city, much broader than the familiar cases of Bedford-Stuyvesant and the South Bronx. The thesis is reminiscent of a Tom Lehrer song, "The Old Dope Peddler," familiar to college students of my vintage, for few areas of the economy, urban or national, seem as conducive to "doing well by doing good as the housing market."

Salins describes housing destruction in New York as a

"problem that clearly transcends housing deterioration, neighborhood 'blight,' inadequate plumbing facilities, dwelling unit disrepair, overcrowding or any other elements of substandard housing . . ." "Indeed," he notes, "apartments and buildings notably free of the classic earmarks of inferior housing . . . succumb to the forces of destruction . . . exhibited in abandonment, arson and the demolition of entire neighborhoods . . . [The destruction seems] to spread in contiguous waves from [its] original epicenters . . . in a pattern quite analogous to the spread of contagious diseases." Conventional explanations of housing abandonment and destruction, Salins argues, are seriously incomplete, because they "are satisfactory only in accounting for the existence or creation of slums, but insufficient to account for the dynamic process in which many of the structures abandoned are in far better condition than housing that retained its market value quite well but a couple of decades ago." The active ecology of housing destruction cannot be accounted for by failures of the private economy, including poverty, code violations, redlining, a rent gap, or filtering. "The outright destruction of the housing stock, as opposed to the existence of substandard dwelling units in poverty neighborhoods, is relatively new, and generally coincides with the amelioration of the worst ravages of poverty through income transfer payments, food stamps, and subsidized health benefits." Moreover, "the destruction significantly exceeds, in number of dwelling units affected or in spatial extent, the size of the city's poverty population."

Thus, rejecting conventional hypotheses, Salins attributes the destruction of housing in New York to an "unfortunate interaction of fragmented and ill-conceived public sector policies" with "a profit-maximizing private real estate industry and a class of housing tenants that understandably pursues its own self-interest." Policies that appear benign in isolation produce starkly perverse effects in the total system. The culprits are many:

The public assistance program, in particular, its administration of the shelter allowance program;

The complex system of rent regulation;

The system of adjudicating landlord-tenant disputes, which seems biased, in its treatment of code complaints, against landlord interests;

The dynamics of real estate ownership of marginal rental properties.

Each of these factors in housing policy, Salins argues, operates "under its own rules, following its own imperatives," a pattern that is "destructive and self-defeating in its larger consequences."

It is not surprising that rent control is the starting point of the argument. The idiosyncratic pattern of rents that rent control produces permits welfare families, with shelter allowances, to range far afield and enter middle class areas. Landlords welcome such turnover because vacancy decontrol permits them to raise rents, and shelter allowances provide them with assurance that rents will be paid, particularly in the increasing number of cases in which payment is made, through two-party checks, on a landlord-tenant basis. Shelter allowances, which are not fungible, vary with family size, providing recipient families with an incentive to maximize housing expenditures. Moving allowances, coupled with the failure of the Welfare Department to reduce the allowance if rent has been withheld, reinforce this. Because the requirement that back rent be paid is linked to the correction of code violations, adjudication of landlord-tenant disputes is biased toward tenants, who have an incentive to create or exaggerate violations. As a result, many tenants turn out to be unevictable and structures that would be viable in a free market become uneconomic.

While investors can purchase properties "in, near, or in the path of the advancing tide of welfare families" at what appear to be bargain prices, they have little value as investment properties. It becomes "progressively harder [for such properties] to attract a non-welfare clientele." Only in the short run can a profitable balance be struck. "A combination of aggressive rent collection efforts, minimal maintenance, tax delinquency, low purchase downpayments, and delinquency in paying off purchase money mortgages can permit an owner to make a handsome profit for a limited time, even as he writes off a larger portion of the rent roll and depreciates the asset value of the property by walking away from his building when its economic potential is exhausted." Occupants of private houses reinforce this as they see the wave of housing destruction approach. Residents "with the means and opportunity to leave" tend to do so and other responsible families [do] not replace them, creating a demand vacuum "that induces desperate . . . (or calculating) landlords to welcome public assistance families, whatever risks they might pose as tenants." The cycle is complete when a neighborhood becomes dominated by public assistance families. At this point "rent delinquency and tenant destructiveness rise and eviction of delinquent tenants becomes difficult, if not impossible. With increasing neighborhood deterioration, even welfare families shun the area and vacancy rates rise. Landlords program their buildings for abandonment, and the epidemic [conquers] another potentially viable section of the city."

Within a decade, Salins points out, 200,000 apartments have been destroyed in New York. "Half of one borough and large parts of two others present such a picture of destruction, that for the entire nation, if not much of the world, these areas and the city that harbors them, epitomize the collapse of urban civilization . . . The most afflicted of these precincts, the South Bronx, is a virtual wasteland and has entered the media's vocabulary as a code-term for terminal urban cancer." All this has occurred despite five decades of concerted public effort at the amelioration of housing conditions ". . . after the city, state and federal government, have poured over $10 billion into the city's housing stock, targeted, mainly, to low and moderate income families . . . and in the face of a public assistance program that picks up the entire rental tab, at levels near the city-wide average, for every eligible low income family in the city, at a cost in excess of $500 million per year."

"However one analyzes it, explains it, describes it or makes apologies for it," Salins concludes, "the ongoing destruction of the city's housing stock is a scandal." The irony and the tragedy is that "this scandal is, in many ways, the product of a basically benign and well-intentioned public sector and a highly regulated and circumscribed private one, a far cry from the laissez-faire indifference and unchecked landlord exploitation that prevailed in the past." Housing policy in New York, short-run in its orientation, has tended to *exacerbate* the weaknesses of the market. Not only is there no evidence that the city has the problem under control, it does not appear to have "accurately diagnosed it."

As remedies, Salins argues that rent-specific housing allowances should be replaced with flat grants, which would, for welfare households, enlarge "the totally discretionary basic living allowance." Rent regulation should be eliminated as apartments are vacated, and the adjudicatory system "must be required to totally divorce considerations of housing maintenance from those of rent delinquency and insure that all proven delinquent tenants can be evicted."

The impact of *The Ecology of Housing Destruction* is dramatic. There is no better summary of its implications than the author's:

> One does not have to be an advocate of laissez-faire, nor an ideological conservative to remark that when it comes to housing in New York, the public sector has done quite enough already. Up to now every new increment of public intervention has made things worse. We have taken so many unsuccessful twists and turns along the path of well-intentioned tinkering that perhaps it is time to test the possibility that generally reasonable incentives and disincentives of an unconstrained market might do a better job of allocating and conserving the housing stock.

The lesson is surely well-taken. One can only hope, for New York's sake, that it can be well-learned.

Harold M. Hochman
Research Director
International Center for Economic Policy Studies
November, 1979

CHAPTER I

CONFRONTING THE PROBLEM

Of all the easily catalogued physical afflictions of New York City the one that receives the greatest attention, and is clearly the most alarming to citizens and public officials alike, is the raging destruction of the housing stock. The South Bronx is often cited as the principal locus of this devastation, but it is only the most egregious example of a syndrome that afflicts many other neighborhoods, some of which are part of the frontier that has advanced outward from the South Bronx. But others are located far from there, elsewhere in the Bronx and in Brooklyn, parts of Manhattan, and even Queens. In the period from 1960 to 1975 it is estimated that over two hundred thousand apartments were lost to the housing stock.

It is a problem that clearly transcends such familiar problems as housing deterioration, neighborhood "blight," inadequate plumbing facilities, dwelling unit disrepair, overcrowding, or any of the other elements in the repertoire of substandard housing conditions. Indeed, as is often noted, apartments and buildings notably free of the classic earmarks of inferior housing can succumb to the forces of destruction. In its extreme manifestation this destruction is exhibited in abandonment, arson, and the demolition of entire neighborhoods and in its intermediate stages, in the selective abandonment, arson, and demolition of individual buildings. Although there are certainly many examples of random or sporadic housing destruction scattered throughout the city, as a general rule the phenomenon seems to spread in contiguous waves from the original epicenters of devastation, in a pattern quite analogous to the spread of contagious diseases. Hence the frequently used metaphor, "epidemic," is not inappropriate.

One of the aspects of the housing destruction syndrome that cannot be emphasized enough is its recency, at least in terms of the magnitude of the problem. The neighborhoods housing most cities' poor people have usually been severely deteriorated, and public and private efforts of amelioration have been only intermittently and partially effective. Although there have always been slums, until the 1960's they were spatially stable and occasioned little housing abandonment or destruction. The frequently noted invasion-succession model describes only the expansion of the slum at its perimeter to accommodate an increase of the poor population. What is new is the phenomenon of, in effect, a rapidly moving slum that razes buildings and neighborhoods in its path. Many of the explanations and theories advanced to explain housing abandonment and destruction are actually satisfactory only in accounting for the existence or creation of slums.

The fate of the housing stock (including any abandonment and destruction) ultimately rests with the private real estate market, and with owners of individual structures in particular. Therefore, the question to be posed is:

If fifteen or more years ago the market valued structures in slum neighborhoods sufficiently highly to permit their owners to retain title to them and maintain them in at least minimally viable condition, regardless of their condition or tenantry, why are owners today turning their back on structures that are in far better condition, and with a tenantry with much greater and more assured rent paying ability?

A Variety of Explanations

The phenomenon of housing destruction and its seeming intractability, especially when it afflicts a housing stock that is still considered sound, baffles planners and public officials charged with stemming the tide. On the other hand, a variety of explanations have been suggested, some of them sophisticated, some of them polemical, but most of them apparently inadequate at least in some respect. The most familiar include:

1. The poverty hypothesis. As in the case of other manifestations of social and economic pathology, there is a school of liberal opinion that will always blame underlying conditions of poverty, discrimination, and neglect. Where we tolerate the existence of a large and permanent underclass of poor and disenfranchised citizens, it is argued, we can only expect a bitter harvest of housing destruction, drug abuse, and crime. The policy corollary of this view is that only by curing the underlying conditions can we deal with the surface manifestations which are only "symptoms."

   A popular counterpart to the liberal view of poverty as prime causal factor stigmatizes all poor or minority families. It assumes that the entire minority or poverty population is destructive, and that any neighborhood that such families enter will eventually be destroyed. The behavioral response implied by this view, to be implemented primarily by individual households and the private sector, is discrimination, segregation, and, if all else fails, flight.

Although there is certainly a very strong correlation between the incidence of poverty and the incidence of housing destruction, the explanation that poverty alone causes the problem is much too simplistic. First, the phenomenon of outright destruction of the housing stock, as opposed to the existence of substandard dwelling units in poverty neighborhoods, is relatively new, and generally coincides with the amelioration of the worst ravages of poverty through income transfer payments, food stamps, and subsidized health benefits. Second, and more important, the phenomenon significantly exceeds, in number of dwelling units affected or in spatial extent, the size of the city's poverty population. Less than 15 percent of the city's population is comprised of the very poor. Yet, at least 25 percent of the city's dwelling units, and a third of its residentially developed land area have been overtaken by the forces of housing destruction.

Aside from its viciousness, the view that the poor are inherently destructive is also unsupported by the evidence. Obviously, the neighborhoods and buildings affected by the destruction syndrome house primarily poor black and Hispanic families. However, poor minority families have lived in New York for generations without having their housing destroyed, and many neighborhoods comprised of poor minority families in New York City and many other

American cities do not witness the problem to any significant degree.

2. The "rent gap" theory. This view is favored by housing economists and academic analysts of the problem. It argues that the rents permitted by rent regulations or constrained by the incomes of the tenantry are lower than the rental income needed to maintain much of the stock, and that the resulting "rent gap" makes many apartment buildings uneconomic, causing their owners to neglect or abandon them. The policy directions suggested by this view include lifting rent regulations and subsidizing tenant rents.

This explanation is in favor at the present time with both public officials and the real estate community. As a consequence, there has been a significant reduction in the restrictiveness of rent regulation, if not in its total extent, and public efforts aimed at increasing tenant subsidies through federal rent supplement programs, as well as changes in the federal regulations affecting public assistance (welfare) shelter allowances.

For all the evident logic and documentation supporting the rent gap theory,[1] it is unsatisfactory as the principal explanation of housing destruction, and consequently the remedies being implemented in its wake will not succeed in solving the problem, whatever other benefits might accrue. Housing destruction has been increasing precisely during the period when, as has been verified by some of the rent gap theorists themselves, the rent gap has been significantly reduced through the relaxation of rent regulation, with the implementation of the maximum base rent program and vacancy decontrol. Furthermore, with many of the tenants in the housing stock at issue relying on public assistance shelter allowances (which are granted independently of other income transfers or living allowances), the poverty population has roughly the same rent paying ability as previous tenants in the buildings affected. If anything, with the high turnover in the welfare population and the relative generosity of the shelter allowance schedules, landlords can increase their rent rolls by renting to poverty (i.e., welfare) families. Finally, it is difficult to argue that, even with inflation, building maintenance costs and taxes alone exceed rent rolls, even under the most restrictive implementation of rent control. As a consequence, the "rent gap," where it has existed, has long ago been capitalized in lower building acquisition costs and does not represent an ongoing burden to the present generation of landlords.

3. The surplus housing hypothesis. Those academic housing analysts and public officials not supporting the rent gap theory generally subscribe to the view that the housing destruction is simply the housing market's way of ridding itself of the most unsatisfactory component of the housing stock in a period of declining demand.[2] This view, allied to the notion of filtering, sees the abandoned, burned, and demolished stock as comprising those dwelling units that have reached the "end of the line," and are in the process of being filtered out of the market altogether. The policy corollary of this view is to let nature run its course, gearing public policy to rapidly ridding the city of all its abandoned structures and making plans for the most effective reuse of the land thus made available.

Some aspects of this view cannot be contested. The supply of housing in New York does exceed the current demand, at least in the boroughs affected by housing destruction, and at some point housing units must eventually leave the stock. However, significant counter arguments can be made to the effect that the housing destruction syndrome itself is responsible for some of the population exodus leading to lowered demand, that the buildings and units being destroyed are not the worst ones in the housing market, and that the extent and pace of destruction far exceed the surplus of housing supply over demand. If market forces continue to keep supply and demand in balance (as opposed to creating a massive housing shortage), this will be due to increased crowding in the areas of resettlement, as families are displaced from destroyed structures, and increased middle class flight from the areas threatened with imminent resettlement by housing refugees. Furthermore, it could be argued that the inferior surplus housing stock would be retired in a much more orderly fashion under healthy housing market conditions.

4. The public sector assumption. Implicit in the city's strategy for rebuilding the South Bronx and adjacent areas is the notion, widely entertained by liberal opinion for over three decades, that the private housing market must fail in poor neighborhoods. A more liberal counterpart to the rent gap theory, this view despairs of the private market's ability to build or maintain housing inexpensive enough for poor families to afford. The major point of departure from the rent gap theory is the belief that such rent gap remedies as rent supplements may not be effective because

they would only enrich landlords, or would be capitalized in higher values for slum real estate, rather than applied to the upgrading or maintenance of the housing stock. The policy remedy inherent in this view is to fund massive public intervention in deteriorated neighborhoods to subsidize the construction or rehabilitation of housing for poor or moderate income families. High quality housing, built and rented under public supervision, would presumably be immune from the forces of housing destruction.

The demolition of the Pruitt-Igoe public housing development in St. Louis in 1974 can be used as a prime counter example to challenge the validity of this perspective. Nevertheless, it can be documented that publicly subsidized housing is, indeed, less apt to fall victim to the syndrome of housing destruction, even in New York City. The premise is unsatisfactory as an explanation of the housing destruction phenomenon, however, because it fails to recognize some of the reasons why, other than rent gaps and landlord rapaciousness, private housing for the poor is more susceptible than publicly assisted housing.

5. Redlining, code violation, and other private market villainies. The easily documented reluctance of banks to invest in deteriorated neighborhoods, or areas adjacent to such neighborhoods, and the exploitative behavior of many apartment building owners are blamed for the process of housing destruction. The policy response to this explanation involves public efforts to require banks to lend in marginal areas, and strict code enforcement, bolstered by publicly sanctioned rent withholding, to

force landlords to maintain proper standards of maintenance.

Attractive and intuitively satisfactory as this explanatory view is, the empirical documentation to support it is weak and contradictory. There is little evidence that the many buildings that have received loans for maintenance or rehabilitation and are situated in zones of housing destruction have been more successful than others in escaping the general devastation. As for code violations, the period of greatest housing destruction coincides with the most stringent (and often successful) efforts of code enforcement, and the most extensive use of court sanctioned rent withholding.

The Ecology of Housing Destruction

Although there are elements of validity in all of the foregoing explanations of housing destruction, the failure of the policies stemming from these views, and the presence of much countervailing empirical evidence, suggest the need for a more conclusive explanation.

There appears to be at work today, in the New York City housing market an active *ecology of housing destruction*, which gains its momentum from the interplay of a number of mutually reinforcing patterns of behavior. Few of these behavioral patterns are, by themselves, especially evil in intent, although some of them are certainly unethical, if not actually illegal. Some of the patterns are initiated, moreover, by well-intentioned public efforts meant to ameliorate housing conditions, at least for individual families. What exists, then, is not a conspiracy, but the unfortunate interaction of fragmented and ill-conceived public sector policies, a profit maximizing private real estate industry, and a class of housing tenants that understandably pursues its own self-interest.

The components of this "ecology of destruction" include:

a. the public assistance (welfare) system, especially with respect to the administration of its program of shelter allowances;
b. the complex, multilayered system of rent regulation and its impact on the market for housing;
c. the system of adjudicating landlord-tenant disputes, especially in its treatment of code violation complaints;
d. the dynamics of the ownership sector of the real estate market, especially as it operates on marginal rental properties.

In each of these components, there is a system that operates under its own rules and follows its own imperatives, where behavior that is logical from the standpoint of internal goals and objectives is destructive and self-defeating in its larger indirect consequences.

The scenario of housing destruction, outlined in the briefest possible way, looks something like this:

At the outset there is a large component of the housing stock that has remained under rent control, with a number of attendant consequences. One is that, even with the capitalization of their depressed rent rolls, many of the structures under rent control will be economically fragile and more susceptible to adverse housing market conditions than unregulated buildings. Another effect is that until 1974 the low (and idiosyncratic) apartment rents in the controlled sector have served to invite poorer families, including those on public assistance (welfare), to roam further afield for housing when they are ready to make a new housing choice, resulting in extensive movement of such households into middle income neighborhoods. The recent decontrol of vacated apartments has not reversed this phenomenon because it makes turnover welcome to landlords, even if the new tenants are technically poorer than their predecessors. Taken by itself this is, of course, not necessarily a negative development. Rigid economic segregation, especially if it is correlated with race, is to be deplored. This infiltration is destructive only because of the way in which it interacts with other systemic effects.

The public assistance system has a significant role in the scenario of housing destruction. Under New York State law, local public assistance agencies may issue to their clients, principally those helped under the Aid to Families with Dependent Children (AFDC) program, a separate allowance for shelter, apart from (and not necessarily correlated with) living allowances. New York City's Department of Social Services (DSS) operates the largest program of shelter allowances in the state, covering over 240,000 families. There is a schedule of maximum permissible rent allowances, which allows larger rents for larger families, and to a limited extent public assistance clients can supplement their shelter allowances with a portion of their basic allowances if they find housing where rents exceed the guidelines. Since a PA family cannot pocket the difference if it occupies accommodations cheaper than the applicable guideline rents, it has an incentive to find the best apartment it can, even if it is more expensive, up to the schedule limit. Because the guideline rents may exceed controlled, or even market, rents in many older New York City neighborhoods, due to a general softness of demand in the housing market in those areas, landlords of marginal buildings with high or growing vacancy rates have an incentive to welcome DSS client families.

Both incentives reinforcing each other intensify the infiltration of poor welfare families into middle class neighborhoods, especially their older or less desirable sections. The regulations under which the DSS operates also permit moving allowances for client families who must, for a variety of reasons, change their place of residence. More significantly, and with devastating effects, welfare families can increase their discretionary incomes and satisfy their desire to move by withholding their rent checks from their landlords. Coupled with the incentive to find the most expensive permissible housing, DSS families have an incentive to move frequently, or at least no incentive not to do so.

The system of adjudicating landlord-tenant disputes, especially those dealing with code violations and rent delinquency is another important factor in the scenario of housing destruction. This system, embodied currently in a multitiered set of administrative and judicial jurisdictions, is most often confronted by two classes of complaints. Landlords appeal to it seeking to evict tenants who are delinquent in their rents, or destructive (of their apartments, of the building, disturbing to other tenants, etc.) or both. Tenants complain of poor maintenance and code violations affecting their apartments or the building in general.

A tendency has developed in recent years for the system to generally give more credence to tenant complaints of code violations than to landlord complaints of rent delinquency and often to balance one complaint against another by making rent collection dependent on the correction of code violations. Rational or symmetrical as such procedures might be in the abstract, there have been very undesirable consequences. The most significant has been that landlords have found much of their tentantry to be unevictable even in the face of massive rent delinquency, and even with respect to irresponsible tenants who continuously wreak a great deal of havoc in their apartments and buildings, ultimately frightening off a more respectable class of tenants, regardless of income. Thus many structures become uneconomic, regardless of theoretical rent rolls, because a large portion of the rents become uncollectable.

Once the pattern has taken hold, moreover, it encourages an ever larger percentage of the poorer tenants to use the landlord-tenant adjudicating process to withhold rents, or simply to harrass their landlords. Even in the case of eviction, the offending family, if it is on welfare, will still receive a shelter allowance, and will be eligible for a moving allowance to boot. For the more calculating families this can create an incentive to be irresponsible, if only to qualify to move. There is no requirement that delinquent welfare tenants under the shelter allowance program must refund to the DSS any allowances not remitted to the landlord, nor can future allowances be effectively garnished to make up rent arrears, nor are such clients seriously in jeopardy of becoming ineligible for further allowances.

Naturally the private real estate market has responded to this set of circumstances. From the point of view of the owners of the housing stock at risk, any apartment buildings that are in, near, or in the path of the advancing tide of welfare families that generally ripples outward in concentric circles from the original poverty epicenters such as Harlem-East Harlem, the South Bronx, and central Brooklyn are not very valuable as investment properties. A prospective purchaser must balance opportunity against risk.

The opportunity resides in acquiring a structure at a very low purchase price, often at least partially decontrolled, with a hypothetical rent roll that can be quite substantial, governed as it is by the rent levels set in the DSS shelter allowance guidelines. The loss of so many dwelling units in the more recently devastated portions of the city temporarily assures, at least among the poor, a healthy demand for apartments, whatever their amenity characteristics. Furthermore, as the tide moves into progressively newer and better neighborhoods, potential purchasers have the opportunity to acquire quite prepossessing structures at bargain prices.

The risks, on the other hand, are also substantial. The welfare families that are most attractive because of DSS shelter allowances are also the most problematical in terms of propensity to pay rents, maintenance of their apartments, responsible social behavior, etc. A landlord must also acknowledge that if his building or the neighborhood accepts many welfare tenants, it will become progressively harder to attract a nonwelfare clientele. The landlord-tenant adjudicatory system will offer little opportunity for redress against delinquent or destructive tenants.

These opportunities and risks can only be effectively balanced profitably in the short run. A strategy has been perfected, by a certain class of real estate operator, of "milking" the marginal housing stock for a short period of time (typically as little as three, and no longer than ten years), and programming their buildings for ultimate abandonment. A combination of aggressive rent collection efforts, minimal maintenance, tax delinquency, low purchase down payments, and delinquency in paying off purchase money mortgages can permit an owner to make a handsome profit for a limited time, even as he writes off a larger portion of the rent roll and depreciates the asset value of the property to zero by walking away from his building when its economic potential is exhausted. Even those owners who have not purchased their structures in order to milk them find themselves falling into this pattern through force of circumstances.

There is also a response in the private housing market

on the demand or consumer side. As they see the wave of housing destruction approach their neighborhoods, many of the families that have the means and opportunity to leave will flee, often well before their area is seriously threatened. Some will move to other neighborhoods of New York City creating demand pressures (and rising rents) in those areas that are still deemed viable because of their distance from the zones of destruction. Others will go to the suburbs. Furthermore, no matter how pleasant these fringe neighborhoods might be, well-founded anxieties for their future will prevent most responsible families from taking the place of those that are fleeing. This creates a demand vacuum that induces desperate (or calculating) landlords to welcome public assistance families, whatever risks they might pose as tenants.

Finally the cycle is complete when the fringe neighborhood gains a growing proportion of public assistance families, many of them irresponsible, fleeing from buildings just recently destroyed. Rent delinquency and tenant destructiveness rises. Eviction of delinquent tenants becomes difficult, if not impossible. With increasing neighborhood deterioration even welfare families shun the area and vacancy rates rise. Landlords program their buildings for abandonment. The epidemic has conquered another potentially viable section of the city.

Slums versus Destruction

In looking at this ecology of housing destruction, it is important to distinguish between those elements that generally have been associated with housing markets geared to poor (and often minority) populations, and those elements that have played a role more recently to insure the actual destruction rather than mere deterioration of the housing stock, in other words, to distinguish between the forces of slum creation and the forces of housing destruction.

The legendary "slum landlord" made a living from providing inferior housing to poor families who had little in the way of housing choice, primarily for economic, but additionally for social reasons.[3] His rental income was low, but so were his expenses. Maintenance was kept at a minimum; labor costs were negligible because the owner managed (and often repaired) his own structure; taxes were low because the building and its neighborhood were in an advanced state of deterioration. Code enforcement was negligible and rent delinquent or destructive tenants could be readily evicted with the cooperation of the judicial system. Because slum buildings were profitable there was a reasonably active market of potential purchasers permitting owners to recoup acquisition and other capital expenditures, and possibly even to realize a capital gain. Slum landlordship was not the bed of roses that the media depicted, but it did represent an economically viable enterprise. Contrary to myth and general perceptions, few slum landlords made fortunes. Most were small marginal entrepreneurs not very different in their backgrounds from their tenants. The buildings and dwelling units were, most likely, execrable; but the meager rent paying ability of the slum tenantry could not support better housing conditions in the private market. (Racial discrimination may have created something of a captive housing market of upwardly mobile minority families who could have afforded better housing outside the slum. Generally, however, the more affluent minority families eventually managed to escape the slum, if not the ghetto.) Inferior as this housing was, it was spatially and physically stable.

With justification, the maintenance of such wretched housing conditions in the midst of the affluence of the majority of the population was increasingly seen to be intolerable by the general public, as well as the slum dwellers themselves. The public sector response to the problem, however, was very limited in extent, and fell far short of the magnitude of the problem. By 1970 the federal government had underwritten 2.8 million units of publicly assisted housing. But there still remained over 8 million substandard units. Nevertheless, the percentage of inferior housing has been consistently declining since the end of World War II because of a reduction in the extent and severity of poverty (largely through an expansion in income transfer payments), and through the process of filtering whereby even the bottom of the market, in terms of demand, has access to an increasingly superior supply because of a rate of housing construction that exceeds the rate of housing deterioration.

New York City, almost alone among the nation's cities, was not content to leave the amelioration of housing conditions to a combination of publicly assisted housing, increased affluence, and the slow workings of the normal "filtering" process. The city, in conjunction with New York State and taking advantage of a number of federal housing programs, has built 331,000 units of publicly assisted housing for low and middle income families, the largest concentration of such housing in the nation and a higher proportion than the population of the city would justify. (Table 1 shows the distribution of rental units by regulatory or subsidized status.) In addition to an unprecedented program of publicly assisted housing the city had developed a tradition of shifting—or more accurately, attempting to shift—the economic burden of providing standard housing at moderate rents to the private ownership sector. It is in this effort, making standard housing available at minimal public cost, that the city has unleashed many of the forces of housing destruction.

Table 1

*Distribution of Rental Units by Regulatory or Subsidized Status,
New York City, 1978*

Status	Number (in 000's)	Percent
Regulated		
Controlled	402	20.8
Pre-1947 stabilized	552	28.6
Post-1947 stabilized	320	16.6
Total	1,274	66.0
Subsidized		
NYC Housing Authority	165	8.6
Other publicly assisted	108	5.6
Total	273	14.2
Not controlled or subsidized	358	18.5
Rooming houses	25	1.3
Total Rental Units	1,930	100.0

Source: U.S. Bureau of the Census

NOTES

1. For the most cogent presentation of the "rent gap" thesis, see Ira S. Lowry, *Rental Housing in New York City, Confronting the Crisis,* the New York City Rand Institute, February 1970, and George Sternlieb and James W. Hughes, *Housing and Economic Reality: New York City 1976,* Center for Urban Policy Research, 1976.
2. While increasingly favored by housing analysts, the "surplus housing" view has been most lucidly expounded in Frank S. Kristof, "Housing Abandonment in New York City," *Conference on Housing, Georgia State University,* 8 May 1966.
3. A good discussion of slum landlordship can be found in George Sternlieb, *The Tenement Landlord* (New Brunswick's Rutgers University Urban Studies Center, 1966).

CHAPTER II

THE HOUSING MARKET

The widespread destruction of the New York City housing stock must be seen in the context of the behavior of the city's housing market. This involves an understanding of the nature of the dynamics of the demand for housing and the concomitant response of the private ownership sector, the city's "landlords." It is tempting to view housing destruction as a social phenomenon or "pathology," the failure of the public sector, the product of capitalist rapaciousness. Actually it is simply the outgrowth of the interplay of quite mundane economic forces of supply and demand; the normal operation of the market place. What have changed, and will continue to change, are the myriad factors that motivate the behavior of housing demanders and housing suppliers. At issue are all the incentives and disincentives, opportunities and risks that become the basis for each housing market actor's own calculations and which, in the aggregate, can create tidal waves that transform the physical face of the city seen in terms of housing construction or abandonment, renovation or neglect.

It is important to be aware of the aggregate constraints on housing market behavior as a backdrop for the detailed consideration of many of these factors. For example, housing demand in New York City as anywhere else is finite and a function of the size of its population. Table 2 indicates the change in the individual and household populations of the city from 1950 through 1975 and projected to 1985. As a result of demographic changes in the age and family status composition of the population, the number of households has declined less rapidly than the population (and may actually increase in the future). Nevertheless, New York's recent population decline has led inexorably to a reduction in households. This by itself has caused the demand for housing to shrink. The fact that housing units have been added to the stock in this period through new construction has simply exacerbated the softness of demand for older, less prepossessing, or less well-situated housing.

Table 2

Population Change in New York City, 1950–1985

Year	Population	Households
1950	7,891,957	2,359,981
1960	7,781,984	2,654,445
1970	7,894,862	2,836,872
1975	7,490,690	2,663,400
1980 (projected)	7,391,510	2,734,859
1985 (projected)	7,231,198	2,747,855

Sources: U.S. Bureau of the Census
Sternlieb and Hughes, "New York City: 1985"

Except for the maintenance of a small vacancy factor, no city can for long sustain a housing stock larger than the number of its households. There is one inescapable conclusion to be drawn from this fundamental fact. Any decline in the number of a city's households, or any housing units added to its housing stock must be balanced by the retirement of a corresponding number of housing units. What is not inevitable, however, is that this shrinkage of the housing stock takes place through abandonment. A number of healthier adjustments can bring housing supply in line with demand. The internal density of structures can be reduced through the consolidation of apartments (as when brownstone rooming houses are converted to one or two family use). The prevailing density of neighborhoods can be reduced through selective redevelopment of specific properties. Residential uses can give way to commercial, institutional or industrial activity. In certain sections of New York City, most notably in Manhattan below 110th Street, all of these things have happened.

Recent Trends in New York City

In spite of the evident potential for a nonpathological decline in the housing stock to match declining demand, neighborhoods of marginal desirability are automatically threatened by any continuing or growing supply-demand gap. This most obvious of generalizations seems to have escaped New York's planners and policy makers in the last decade. More than 470,000 units have been added to the city's stock since 1960. Even if we discount private sector construction as lying outside the reach of public policy (which is not really the case), the public sector alone contributed over 90,000 units during this period.

As much of the publicly subsidized housing was meant to appeal to, and be afforded by, the city's middle and lower middle income families, it could only be tenanted at the expense of the less desirable apartments in the less desirable buildings in deteriorating neighborhoods. Furthermore, while private construction has generally proceeded in small increments, permitting a gradual adjustment in the units affected by the "vacancy chain" of moves, the publicly assisted developments have involved enormous additions to the housing stock which have had to be absorbed over very short periods. In addition to such earlier projects as Trump Village in Brooklyn, with 4,281 units completed in 1964, and Rochdale Village in Queens, whose 5,860 units were completed in 1965, Co-op City in the Bronx with 25,372 units was completed between 1965 and 1972, and Starrett City in Brooklyn with 5,888 units was completed in 1976. These abrupt enlargements of housing supply in a period of demographically based declining demand caused a "siphon" effect as many residents of older structures were sucked into the new developments causing rashes of vacancies to suddenly erupt throughout the city, but especially in its most vulnerable neighborhoods.

Although it has been argued that the new housing construction provided an in-city alternative for families that otherwise would have left New York, in fact much of this housing was ultimately occupied by families who would have been unable or unwilling to pay for housing in the suburbs. Indeed, the construction of these "shallow" subsidy developments was justified as a remedy for those families ineligible for "deep" subsidy public housing but priced out of the private market. It should be noted in passing that over 25 percent of the stock built with public subsidies in this period are now in financial trouble, unable to meet their mortgage and tax obligations. These financially troubled developments would be solvent, of course, if their rents were raised, but for reasons very much related to some of the components of the ecology of housing destruction, this is politically impossible.

As the most casual perusal of the city's housing geography will confirm, the impact of declining housing demand was and remains highly selective. As of 1975 the city wide vacancy rate was approximately 2.9 percent. Among the five boroughs it varied as follows: Bronx, 3.4 percent; Brooklyn and Manhattan, 2.8 percent; Queens; 1.3 percent and Staten Island, 2.1 percent. These figures are grossly misleading and understate the magnitude of declining demand, however, because abandoned units are not included in the vacancy totals. More accurate indicators of the variations in housing demand within the city might be recent changes in household population, and recent changes in rent levels (to the degree permitted by rent regulation).

Citywide, the total number of households declined by 3.8 percent between 1965 and 1975. The boroughs vary in this respect much more than they did in vacancy rates, with Manhattan and the Bronx experiencing a decline of approximately 10 percent, and Brooklyn 6.7 percent, at the same time that Queens increased its household population by 17.7 percent and Staten Island by 41.7 percent. Such data on recent population change do not accurately reflect the degree to which decline or growth of housing demand reflects the intrinsic desirability of an area, as opposed to the effects of competition among residential and nonresidential land uses or the degree to which housing density is declining in nonpathological ways. The similarity of the Manhattan and Bronx population decline figures are especially misleading in this respect. An index that might complement the population data would reflect recent increases in rent relative to the city as a whole. The citywide median rent increase rate per apartment between 1965 and 1975 was 101.2 percent. It varied among the boroughs significantly, ranging from a low of 88.3 percent in Queens through 91.4 percent in the Bronx, 97.6 percent in Brooklyn, 116.0 percent in Manhattan, to a high of 125.0 percent in Staten Island. Since Queens and Staten Island experienced significant population increases during this period, and most of the Staten Island stock is owner occupied, their rent increase figures are not especially relevant indices of weak or strong housing demand. Much more significant are the Bronx, Brooklyn, and Manhattan comparisons which indicate that among these boroughs only Manhattan experienced a nonpathological decline in housing demand. More accurately stated, Manhattan alone among these three, at least outside of Harlem and East Harlem, experienced a decline in housing supply with an attendant displacement of households, predominantly the poorer ones.

Even within each of the five boroughs, rates of demand decline (or growth) have varied considerably from one neighborhood to the other. As a rough generalization we have witnessed the severe decline (in demand and neighborhood desirability) of the entire southern and eastern portions of the Bronx, the northern and eastern areas of Brooklyn, southeastern Queens, and upper Manhattan. Conversely, increases in housing demand and relative neighborhood desirability have been experienced in the Riverdale section of the Bronx, southern Brooklyn, northeastern Queens and central Manhattan. Staten Island has remained *sui generis*, a burgeoning middle and lower middle income suburb trapped within the city's municipal boundaries.

Spatial Dynamics

The most important aspect of housing market behavior in any city is the dynamic of spatially shifting patterns of demand, viewed in terms of the income, ethnic, and family characteristics of the demanders, and the attendant changes in the quality or desirability of neighborhoods affected by these shifts. To some extent all American cities are continually subject to vast citywide games of residential "musical chairs," with the "players" representing the various demand sectors and the "chairs" the various neighborhoods. In trying to explain or retard housing and neighborhood deterioration, the burden of analysis falls on attempts to determine why "players" are changing seats, who is going where, and what is happening to the characteristics of the "chairs" in the process. In a subsequent chapter, the behavior of the owners of the "chairs," and their contribution to the game will be analyzed.

Regarding the dynamics of housing destruction in New York, although New York's housing market is by no means unique among American cities either in its weaknesses or its strengths, much of the housing destruction is related to distortions in the spatial dynamics of residential location behavior that can be attributed to, or have been exacerbated by, policies or institutions that are unique to the city. The peculiarities of these spatial dynamics can be illuminated most effectively by comparing the normal operations and expectations of housing markets in other American cities to those of New York. To the degree that other American cities have experienced their version of the "musical chairs" game, and their own pathologies of housing abandonment and destruction, these can be attributed to the interactions of a triad of circumstances: an excess of housing supply over demand, the dynamics of filtering, and racial change.

As was indicated earlier, any continuing excess of housing supply over demand must result in the eventual retirement of the excess stock. There are three relevant factors to be examined in any city faced with an apparent surplus of housing. One is the degree to which the surplus results from a metropolitanwide supply-demand imbalance, where the central city loses residents to its suburbs. Another is the market's verdict as to which central city structures or neighborhoods will be retired. The third is whether the retirement of units is through abandonment or through such presumably preferable adaptations as structural conversions or reuse of sites and structures for nonresidential activities.

In a classic filtering model, the entire metropolitan area functions as a single integrated housing market.[1] All housing units are graded in terms of their intrinsic desirability, on the basis of conditions and amenities pertaining to the unit, its structure, or its location. The greater the quality of the unit the more expensive. This supply hierarchy is mirrored in an income stratified set of housing demanders. All households try to occupy the best housing they can afford, with the most affluent getting the best housing and the poorest, the worst. As the metropolitan housing demand declines relative to supply, either through the construction of new housing or through population decline, the least desirable units will drop out of the market.

Certain assumptions are built into this model. One is that newer housing is generally of higher quality than older, so in combination with the general tendency of newer housing to locate farther from the metropolitan central business district, this assumption erects the premise that the most undesirable housing will generally be in the center of the metropolitan area and that therefore most of the obsolete housing will be in the central city rather than the suburbs. Another assumption is that the process is benign because all housing demanders can acquire better units at no increase in price when there is a housing surplus. Implicit in the filtering model is the understanding that the maximum number of housing units at risk in any metropolitan area will be equal to the excess of supply (the entire metropolitan stock) over demand (all metropolitań households) minus a small vacancy factor (say 5 percent). Also implicit in the filtering model, and this must be emphasized, is a fixed hierarchical order among units, structures, and neighborhoods in terms of their desirability, with all units eventually taking their place at the bottom of the pecking order of desirability.

As will be developed, the classic filtering model is entirely inadequate to explain the destruction of housing in New York City. The housing literature indicates that the model is inappropriate to most other American cities as well because of the operation of one of the most fundamental locational forces of American urban experience: neighborhood racial change.[2] Housing economists have finally discovered what all American families have always known. Although the physical characteristics of units, structures and neighborhoods are important, nothing matters as much in a family's choice of housing as the characteristics of their prospective neighbors. In this respect the social class of a neighborhood's residents is a fundamental factor in determining the spatial patterns of housing demand. Because class is largely a function or reflection of income, the classic filtering model predicts a large degree of spatial segregation by class, and intra-neighborhood class homogeneity.

Given the overlap in the income distributions of white and minority families, however, even though the average minority family's income is a third less than that of the average white family, the class segregation of the filtering model does not necessarily, by itself, insure racial segregation or intra-neighborhood racial homogeneity. Nevertheless, race is even more important to most white families than social class. This is because of the nearly universal expectation of white families that minority occupied neighborhoods will eventually become minority dominated, and that this will cause property values (important to owner residents) to decline. Therefore, white families, regardless of income, seem unwilling for long to live in areas with a large proportion of minority families, regardless of their income, ultimately causing their expectations to be fulfilled.

Where minority families have been able to penetrate white neighborhoods, even when this has occurred through the normal dynamics of filtering, the demand among white families has collapsed with a number of attendant consequences. The relative pecking order of neighborhoods in terms of desirability has been altered such that minority-occupied areas of previously higher desirability fall behind most white areas, regardless of their amenity levels. This has forced a downward adjustment in the average price of housing in minority occupied areas which ultimately insures their occupancy by families with lower incomes than the previous inhabitants. White families leaving such areas (or the ones that would previously have taken their place) will not settle for inferior housing elsewhere in the metropolitan area, so that the better their neighborhood was before minority families moved in, the more likely that they can only find superior white neighborhoods further from the center of the metropolitan area. Usually this has meant crossing the boundary from central city to suburb. The forces of racial change thus become the major factor distorting, but not completely invalidating, the filtering model in most American cities.

There is another problem with the filtering model as well. Excessive weight is placed on the age of housing, neglecting two other important characteristics: the initial design quality, and the level of continuing maintenance. The supply of new housing is not oriented exclusively to the most affluent households. New homes are built for a variety of classes ranging from the lower middle to the highest. The higher the target class of any new dwelling unit, the longer it will survive in the housing stock as a desirable one. A variant of this phenomenon is the fact of changing standards of design and construction over time. There has been a secular decline in the quality of residential design and construction that makes much of the older stock more attractive than newer houses and apartments. Independent of these factors, but often related to them, housing units can sustain their desirability indefinitely if they are properly maintained and modernized. These several exceptions to the filtering model can be reconciled within the framework of the "sectoral" hypothesis.[3] The various social classes of a metropolitan area are arrayed in a set of pie-shaped sectors emanating from the central business district. The quality of the housing stock varies significantly by sector, both in terms of design and maintenance along the lines indicated above. However, within each sector something like the classic filtering process takes place, tempered, as described, by the dynamics of racial succession.

The process of racial change and the sectorally differentiated qualitative dimension, when added to the filtering model, provide a theoretical framework which can offer hypotheses as to the consequences of a supply-demand imbalance in a metropolitan housing market. In metropolitan areas with small minority populations a number of alternative outcomes could be foreseen depending on the relative rates of metropolitan population housing growth. If the metropolitan population has grown, but not as rapidly as its housing stock, the oldest low quality stock near the center of the metropolitan area (in the lower class "sector") would be retired. The growth of the metropolitan area would, however, justify an expansion of the central business district so that these areas of obsolete housing would be redeveloped (or converted) for commercial activities. If the metropolitan population has not grown, still assuming a housing supply surplus, there might be abandonment of the obsolete housing adjacent to the central business district, or its replacement by parking lots and other low intensity uses. In either case, the high amenity inner city housing would probably be maintained or alternately neglected and "gentrified" (colonized by the upper middle class) at periodic intervals. The metropolitan areas of Portland, Minneapolis, and Denver seem to fall within the former pattern, while the metropolitan areas of Boston, Duluth, and Pittsburgh exemplify the latter.

Metropolitan areas with large minority populations, virtually all the larger American ones, would display a somewhat different scenario. An excess of housing supply over demand will permit widespread infiltration of minority families into adjacent white, often medium to high quality, neighborhoods. Racial change and housing turnover in these neighborhoods will be extremely rapid, creating a demand vacuum. In other words, white families will leave at a more rapid rate than minority families can take their place.

The process does not even require white "flight," as the term is usually used. Even a normal, orderly, departure rate of white families can have this effect if no whites can be found to take their place. While the demand vacuum will be most extreme at the center of the impacted neighborhood, ripple effects of nonreplaced white outmigration will be felt at the edge of the area as well.

This process of racial succession followed by a demand vacuum can accelerate as it becomes self reinforcing. The outmigration of white families can create a market for new housing elsewhere in the metropolitan area, exacerbating the supply-demand imbalance. If the "invaded" neighborhoods experience a significant degree of abandonment as a result of the sudden collapse in demand, this will encourage minority movement into adjacent areas. These areas will be able to accommodate them because of high vacancy rates occasioned by anticipatory white flight.

The role of housing prices in the process is very important. To expand the region of minority occupancy, ever poorer families have to be enticed by the local housing market. This requires a downward adjustment in the price of the housing stock or an upward adjustment in the rent-paying propensity of the poor minority households. Both of these adjustments take place. Rapid white flight and lowered expectations of future property values force a lowering of housing prices, while shortages of housing caused by abandonment in the center or leeward side of the affected region are reflected in a competitive bidding up of rents by minority families. The process stabilizes, and a new perimeter of minority occupancy is established when minority families can no longer significantly improve their housing by penetrating further into white neighborhoods, or the price of doing so exceeds the increment of quality that is gained.

The degree to which the process creates abandonment depends on a number of factors. Obviously the size of the supply-demand gap and the size of the reservoir of minority families plays an important role. The greater either of these variables is the more extreme and rapid the pace of neighborhood racial change, and the potential for abandonment. The location of impacted neighborhoods is also significant. If these areas are adjacent to the central business district, and the metropolitan population is growing, commercial expansion can absorb much of the territory of vacated housing. Alternatively, if there is an insignificant amount of commercial expansion, and/or the impacted region is far from the central business district, the rate and degree of abandonment can be extensive, causing the central business district itself to deteriorate in the process.

Although the prior discussion has heavily emphasized

the racial aspect of this dynamic, there is considerable disagreement among housing economists as to the relative
weight of race and income in triggering the process of
neighborhood deterioration.[4] The proponents of the view
that class is more important than race will point to the
large number of solidly middle class minority families or,
conversely, the large number of very poor whites to be
found in any American metropolitan area as proof that: (a)
race and class are not necessarily always correlated with
each other, and by extension; (b) middle class minority
families will not adversely affect a neighborhood while
poor white families will.

However, two factors make race more important than
class, at least in initiating the dynamics described above.
These can be summarized in the statement that the housing market operates to minimize the possibility of initial
non-race related income integration, or blunts its impact if
it does occur, while it increasingly permits racial integration without diminishing its historical destabilizing influence.

First, as was noted, the normal operation of the housing
market through differential housing prices usually insures
enough segregation by income to keep the process of income group succession limited to the normal downward
filtering of obsolete or undesirable housing so that non-
race related penetration of middle class areas by poor families will rarely occur. If, in a free housing market, low
income families move into stable middle or high income
neighborhoods without public subsidies, the phenomenon
will be extremely limited in extent and these families, by
the very fact of the ability to "afford" the higher priced
housing, will be accepted as de facto middle class.

Isn't this view contradicted by the existence of neighborhoods that are heterogeneous in the price of their hous-

ing? No, because such areas can be explained by one of three eventualities. One is that middle class occupancy will continue in the area because of locational or other amenities accruing to it and because its class heterogeneity is already accepted. This is the case in many desirable sections in or near the central business districts of most larger central cities. Another is that the demand for housing in the area on the part of the middle class is strong enough to wipe out any prior supply price disparities, either through an upgrading of the originally lower priced units, or the ability to secure high prices for presumably "inferior" ones. This is also frequently the case in centrally located "fashionable" districts. Or the price disparities are reflective of a downward filtering in progress, and the middle class families represent a transitory and diminishing demand segment.

The other factor making racial integration more destabilizing than income integration is the paradoxical result of the increase in housing purchasing power among minority families. Many minority families are obviously middle class, and they can afford to move to middle class white neighborhoods. Nevertheless, they are perceived as the cutting edge of eventual low income minority domination. This belief on the part of white families and the housing lending establishment creates a self-fulfilling prophecy. This "problem" has always existed but its impact was limited as long as blatant racial discrimination in housing was condoned and practiced. The passage of at least somewhat effective fair housing legislation and increased levels of superficial racial tolerance have weakened the barriers to minority infiltration. Of course, if racial tolerance increases to any significant degree, reducing the negative expectation of whites regarding minority occupied neighborhoods, the demand vacuum need never arise.

Applying the Model to New York City

This cursory review of normal housing market processes, seen primarily from the perspective of spatial patterns of demand, has been introduced to provide a context for viewing the New York City experience. Clearly the New York metropolitan area is an example of the housing surplus, large minority population prototype. It is not alone. The metropolitan areas of Chicago, Detroit, St. Louis, Newark, and Cleveland, to name only a few, display similar profiles. Changes in the New York City housing market, including the high levels of abandonment and housing destruction, are to a large extent manifestations of the market operations outlined above.

However, New York is unique in one important respect: the degree of public intervention in the housing market. It can be argued fairly persuasively that the magnitude of housing destruction in New York City far exceeds what the normal market processes would generate, even under the most adverse of circumstances, and that this excess housing destruction is related to the various components of what was described in the introduction as the "ecology of housing destruction." Table 3 indicates approximate levels of cumulative abandonment in those metropolitan areas that have experienced it to any degree, and relates these levels to the magnitude of recent population loss. New York stands out in the ratio of abandonment to population loss, being surpassed in this regard by only two other cities.

As a matter of fact, New York's ratio of housing supply to demand, the geographical extent of the metropolitan area, and its high proportion of rental housing should have

Table 3

Housing Abandonment and Household Loss
Selected American Cities, 1965-1975

City	Estimated Cumulative Abandonment	Estimated Household Loss	Abandonment/ Household Loss Ratio
New York City	199,000	82,259	2.42
Chicago, Ill.	64,500	96,416	0.67
Detroit, Mich.	62,000	63,921	0.97
Philadelphia, Pa.	33,161	48,031	0.69
St. Louis, Mo.	30,250	34,740	0.87
Newark, N.J.	23,462	13,040	1.80
Camden, N.J.	14,500	4,763	3.04
East St. Louis, Ill.	13,650	4,260	3.20
Cleveland, Ohio	11,675	40,031	0.29
Cincinnati, Ohio	6,750	14,625	0.46
Buffalo, N.Y.	3,350	19,860	0.17

Sources: U.S. Bureau of the Census
Author's analysis of housing and vacancy data for selected American cities

served to yield a lower than normal amount of housing destruction under free market conditions. The vacancy rate in New York City's housing stock has never been as high as that of other older eastern cities. The vastness of the metropolitan area should normally reduce the propensity or ability of many middle class families to leave the city. The high proportion of renters (as Table 4 indicates, almost three quarters of the city's population are tenants, either in apartment houses or two to five family houses) should make expectations of property value decline less important, at least on the demand side. A large middle class minority population should have been able to fill much of the vacuum left by departing whites.

Table 4

Distribution of Dwelling Units by Structure Type,
New York City, 1978

Dwelling Unit Type	Number (in 000's)	Percent
Apartment houses		
Old law tenement	186	6.6
New law tenement	575	20.4
Post-1929	712	25.3
Total	1,473	52.4
Two–Five family houses		
Owner-occupied	383	13.6
Renter-occupied	607	21.6
Total	990	35.2
One-family houses		
Owner, occupied	307	10.9
Renter, occupied or vacant	42	1.5
Total	349	12.4
Total dwelling units	2,812	100.0

Source: U.S. Bureau of the Census

New York's disproportionate incidence of housing destruction can be explained by identifying some of the factors that differentiate it from the other high-minority, slack-demand prototypes:

1. Typically neighborhood class changes slowly because it is initiated by racial change manifested in the penetration of middle class minority families into middle class white neighborhoods. Only later may poor minority families settle in their wake. In New York neighborhood class change takes place instantly because of the interaction of depressed rent levels (the result of rent control) and housing-

subsidized poor families (the welfare shelter allowance program).

2. Typically the spatial extent of neighborhood class change stabilizes as poor families can no longer improve their housing except at much higher rents and landlords or owners can no longer fill their vacancies except at much lower prices. In New York all poor families have the same rent paying ability (because of welfare shelter allowances) and one that is competitive with the rent paying ability of the lower middle class.

3. Typically the demand vacuum results from a market-based surplus of housing supply over demand resulting from normal population decline. New York's demand vacuum has resulted from an abnormally high rate of publicly assisted middle income housing construction at the same time that rapid neighborhood class change has precipitated an abnormally high rate of middle class flight.

Subsequent chapters will try to describe the various components of the ecology of destruction that have resulted in a disproportionate rate of housing destruction and that have made New York notorious among American cities as an example of physical devastation.

NOTES

1. The filtering literature is extensive. Some landmark discussions of the concept include Richard U. Ratcliff, *Urban Law and Economics* (New York: McGraw-Hill, 1949); Fisher and Winnick, "A Reformulation of the Filtering Concept," *Journal of Social Issues* 7 (1951), pp. 47-85; Ira S. Lowry, "Filtering and Housing Standards," *Land Economics* 36 (November 1960) pp. 362-370.
2. Charles L. Levin et. al., *Neighborhood Change, Lessons in the Dynamics of Urban Decay* (New York: Praeger, 1976).

3. Peter D. Salins, "Household Location Patterns in American Metropolitan Areas," *Economic Geography*, 47: 2 (June 1971) pp. 234-248.
4. Levin, *Neighborhood Change.*
5. Amount for fiscal year 1978.

CHAPTER III

WELFARE HOUSING ALLOWANCES

The biggest housing assistance program in New York City is the shelter allowance system of the City's Department of Social Services. As of 1978, 242,000 public assistance (welfare) clients received stipends to cover the full cost of their shelter rents. In sheer volume this dwarfs the inventory of apartments managed by the New York City Housing Authority (165,000 units), the sum of all other publicly assisted housing units ever built (166,000 units), or federally financed rent supplements (15,000 per year). As a stipend specifically earmarked for housing expenses, and not fungible for any other purpose, the shelter allowance should not be treated simply as a component of income maintenance. It is as much a housing subsidy as the output of other public programs which either underwrite a portion of the costs of housing construction, or which bridge the gap between a tenant's rent paying capability and market rents. The problem has been, however, that everyone has viewed the shelter allowances as an income maintenance rather than a housing assistance effort. As a result even with an annual expenditure of $557 million,[1] most of the 242,000 recipient households are nevertheless wretchedly housed, the housing markets in the neighborhoods where public assistance families have settled have been distorted, and the neighborhoods themselves have been severely destabilized, if not destroyed.

Although not unique to New York City and New York State, the issuance of a non-fungible housing allowance geared to rent-as-paid is maintained as an administrative practice in only three other states. The arguments regarding the degree to which income maintenance payments should allow their recipients' discretion, as opposed to being earmarked for specific expenditure categories, go to the heart of the philosophy of public assistance. The social welfare and public assistance "establishment" has been clearly ambivalent on this point.

On the one hand, social welfare orthodoxy eschews paternalism and insists that public assistance recipients should be as free as all other citizens in organizing their lives and spending their money. In the service of this view, progressively fewer "strings" have been attached to public assistance grants over the years, and the direct supervision of recipients has steadily declined. This may have been largely related to the desire to reduce the bureaucratic costs and effort associated with paternalistic policies, but it has certainly been congruent with social welfare ideology.

On the other hand, the social welfare professsionals have not really trusted their clientele to behave responsibly. "What if a welfare recipient squanders money on unnecessary expenditures, doesn't buy enough food, doesn't set aside enough for rent?" Thus the foundation was laid for the once widespread practice of reducing the welfare recipient's economic discretion by apportioning the allowance among a variety of expenditure categories. As of 1978, most states had, however, collapsed all such allowances into flat grants that differed only in terms of household size and need. The remaining states, including New York,

Table 5

*States Issuing Separate Shelter Allowances
to Public Assistance Recipients, 1976*

| State | Form of Shelter Allowance | |
	Flat Grant	Rent Specific
Connecticut		X
Hawaii	X	
Indiana		X
Kansas	X	
New York		X
South Dakota	X	
Vermont		X

Source: U.S. HEW, *Characteristics of State Plans for Aid to
Families with Dependent Children,* 1976

collapsed most categories into the living allowances but kept the shelter allowance separate, non-fungible and tied to documented levels of rent payment rather than basing it on family characteristics.

The Way the System Works

The impact of a shelter allowance program on the housing market depends on the way it is designed and administered. In New York City, all public assistance recipients are eligible for the shelter allowance, with the amount of the allowance dependent on a state determined schedule of *maximum* rents that varies among regions of the state.

The scheduled maximums vary with the size and composition of the recipient household. Table 6 indicates the present and recent rent allowance ceilings in current and constant dollar terms. There is some disagreement as to the degree to which the schedule ceilings are really fixed. In a 1977 report of the New York State comptroller, it was asserted that 23.6 percent of allowances exceeded schedule maximums. The present administrator of the program insists, however, that there are only a negligible number of allowances that exceed the scheduled limits at the present time.[2] The schedule has been raised from time to time, but as the data indicate, not as rapidly as the consumer price index for housing. Whether or not recipients can appeal the scheduled rent ceilings, they are free to pay more than the scheduled amount if they are willing to make up the difference out of their pocket as long as they do not divert more than 15 percent from their living allowance. At the present time only a small percentage of all recipients are known to pay rents exceeding the schedule.

The shelter allowance checks, which are distributed bimonthly, are mailed to the welfare households and made out in the name of the household head. This means that the recipient may, if she or he wishes, cash the check and use it for non-rent purposes. If the landlord complains to DSS of non-payment of rent, he may be eligible for a restricted or "two-party" check; that is a check made out jointly to the welfare client and the landlord. Federal regulations have always severely limited the percentage of two-party shelter allowance checks that are eligible for maximum federal reimbursement under the federal-state-city cost sharing formula. Under a great deal of pressure from the New York City government and congressional delegation, in 1977 HEW acceded to an increase in the proportion of two-party checks from the previous ceiling of 10 percent to a new limit of 20 percent. Even before this

administrative change, New York City frequently exceeded the federal guideline, and thus forfeited a significant amount of federal reimbursement.

Table 6

*AFDC Shelter Allowance Ceilings
in Current and Constant (1968) Dollars,
New York City, 1959-1979*

Number of Family Members	Maximum Monthly Allowance								
	Current Dollars				Constant (1968) Dollars				
	1959	1969	1971	1975	1959	1969	1971	1975	1979
1	65	75	100	152	76	68	79	91	72
2	75	85	100	183	88	77	79	110	87
3	75	85	125	194	88	77	99	116	92
4	95	105	125	218	111	95	99	131	104
5	95	105	125	226	111	95	99	136	107
6	100	115	135	249	117	104	107	149	118
7	100	125	160	303	117	113	127	187	144
8	110	125	160	317	129	113	127	190	151
9	110	135	175	317	129	122	139	190	151

Source: New York City Human Resources Administration

There are only limited sanctions applied by DSS against
rent delinquent welfare households. If the city wide quota
of two-party checks is not exhausted the agency will settle
a case of rent delinquency by putting the household on a
two-party check. If rent delinquency results in eviction,
the household will still be eligible for a shelter allowance
in its new apartment. Under no circumstances does rent
delinquency make the welfare household ineligible for further public assistance. Its living allowance may be "garnished" by a very small amount, but never at a level that
can provide restoration to either the landlord or the
agency. If a rent delinquent household complains that the
check was stolen, or never received, it will receive another
check (as would be the case with the living allowance as

well), with only a minimum of DSS investigation of the facts.

Public assistance households are expected to find their own housing, although DSS personnel may be helpful in a variety of ways. If a family is displaced by fire, abandonment, or other urgent reasons, the household's caseworker is responsible for helping the family find alternative housing, even if only temporarily. Under such circumstances, the guidelines might be violated, presumably only briefly, if, for example, hotels would have to be utilized. More generally, DSS can refer clients to known or potential vacancies and can intercede on their behalf if any obstacles to securing an apartment are encountered. Thus, while DSS does not exactly run a housing placement service, its clients receive a great deal more placement assistance than the population at large. Again, while DSS personnel have no grand strategy as to where their clients should live, generally pursuing their housing placement responsibilities in terms of opportunity and expediency, consciously or not, they do act to "steer" the public assistance population into certain neighborhoods.

Public assistance households are permitted to move, of course, and are eligible for a "moving allowance." A recent report [3] has estimated that 20 percent of the welfare population moves every year. The 1978 official city housing survey shows that 28.5 percent of welfare tenants moved into their present apartment within the previous year. Because they have tended to move a great deal for a variety of reasons (some of which are germane to the ecology of destruction), there has been a tightening of the rules regarding moving allowances. Before 1976, welfare families could move as often as they wished, receiving a moving allowance each time. After that year, DSS adopted rules that permit families to move only once every two years, unless they are displaced by forces beyond their control. In many ways the system operates to create significant incentives for public assistance households to move, and very few disincentives. The two most important incentives include the desire to cash the rent checks and use the proceeds for other expenditures, and the desire to secure a better apartment. In many instances these two objectives can be pursued jointly.

Tenant Strategies

The most calculating kind of welfare household will become rent delinquent in order to increase its income, and it can establish a legitimate justification to move at the same time. The period of rent delinquency yields the family a higher income. When the landlord's patience is exhausted he will ask to have the tenant placed on a two-party check, or barring that, will attempt to evict the family by undertaking legal dispossess proceedings. When (or if) the landlord succeeds in the eviction, the family, being officially dispossessed of its apartment, will be eligible to move under DSS guidelines, regardless of the length of occupancy since the last move. DSS may even have to help it find a new apartment. If the family wishes to extend the period of rent delinquency it can complain to the housing court of code violations. Given the complexity of the housing code and the probable deteriorated conditions of the apartment or building, it should not be difficult to document code violations. In the unlikely event that no legitimate code violations exist, the family can create some. With legal assistance, a determined family can forestall eviction for a considerable period, pocketing its shelter allowance the entire time. For the unscrupulous welfare family, this represents a "no-lose" strategy. The only potential sanction for rent delinquency is eviction, and this is perceived as an opportunity to occupy a better apartment, rather than punishment.

Even the more responsible welfare household can find itself playing this game. Such a household may find a more desirable apartment through its own exertions. It has significant incentives to do so. It may not be currently renting at the guideline maximum, or increased family size may make it eligible for a larger allowance, and there will always be "better" apartments beyond the zone of welfare occupancy, especially as the pace of neighborhood deterioration and abandonment accelerates. In the interval that elapses between the time it makes a commitment to take the new apartment and the date of occupancy, it will have no incentive to pay the rent to its present landlord, or to make up any accumulated arrears. Whatever the motivation or the circumstances, rent delinquency among the welfare population is staggering. The most recent official estimate is 36 percent, and many knowledgeable persons believe that this figure is far too conservative.[4]

Of course, an absolutely indispensable factor in making these rent delinquency strategies possible is the willingness of landlords to accept welfare families in spite of documented or suspected previous rent delinquency. Why would landlords do this? In the most extreme cases, the owners of deteriorated structures in partially devastated neighborhoods have no choice. The alternative to welfare families is a high vacancy rate, and even welfare families willing to move in may be hard to come by. In other cases landlords find that the shelter allowance guidelines are more generous than the prevailing market rents. Increasingly, however, landlords will accept previously rent delinquent families only under a two-party check arrangement.

Since the enlarged HEW quota for two-party checks of 20 percent has not yet been exhausted, any otherwise unwelcome rent delinquent families can secure acceptance somewhere, by entering into a two-party check agreement with a landlord. The two-party check can also be a remedy for rent delinquency in a welfare family's existing building. Any landlord complaining to DSS of a rent delinquent tenant can have that tenant transferred to a two-party check account after a single missed payment. Should the 20 percent quota be exhausted the city would undoubtedly press, perhaps successfully, for further enlargement of the quota, or would be willing to absorb the full cost of shelter allowances exceeding the quota.

Two-Party Checks

Many public officials and real estate industry spokesmen see the two-party check arrangement as a panacea, and its expanded use as a major factor in stemming the tide of abandonment.[5] This view is founded on the assumption that landlords abandon their buildings principally because widespread rent delinquency makes them uneconomic, and that the major problem that landlords of buildings predominantly tenanted by welfare recipients face is rent delinquency. What is not recognized is the role that welfare shelter allowances in general, and two-party checks in particular, play as incentives for welfare households to become more mobile and irresponsible than they would otherwise be.

The fact to be addressed is this: welfare households under two-party check arrangements are much more apt to move than other welfare or nonwelfare households. One can assume that the lessening of risk entailed by landlords who accept welfare tenants with two-party checks will make such tenants more acceptable than they would be otherwise. Given any slackness at all in the housing market in the neighborhoods on the "better" side of any concentration of welfare families (a slackness precipitated by the nonreplacement of nonwelfare families because of the anticipation of neighborhood change), many welfare families will have an incentive to seek a better apartment. The possibility of a two-party check arrangement removes the major obstacle to their obtaining such an apartment. In the aggregate these dynamics assure rising vacancy rates in the less desirable areas being left behind. Rising vacancy rates then pose an even greater threat to affected landlords than rent delinquency. In desperation such landlords will accept even the largest families or the most irresponsible ones, eventually driving out the more respectable tenants, even those on welfare. This will assure abandonment as well as the forced relocation (into presumably "better" neighborhoods) of the remaining tenantry.

This line of reasoning could be challenged only if the welfare rent schedule contained ceilings well below market rents, so that even armed with two-party checks, welfare households would be priced out of the better apartment vacancies. As it stands, however, the DSS rent schedule is fairly congruent with market rents. For the city as a whole the median welfare rent is only twenty-five dollars less than the nonwelfare median. In the neighborhoods at risk there is either apt to be no differential or welfare guidelines may surpass market rent levels. Furthermore, non-welfare tenants have a much greater incentive to bargain with landlords and resist rent increases than households on welfare who stand to gain nothing by paying rents below the stipulated ceilings. Hence we can be reasonably certain that the welfare tenantry is not being priced out of the rental market in areas adjacent to present concentrations of welfare families.

The only other constraint on welfare tenant mobility is the DSS regulation specifying a minimum interval of two years between moves. This constraint can be circumvented by a determined welfare household in a variety of ways. It can invite eviction through any number of kinds of disruptive or destructive behavior. (This may be manifested not

Table 7

*Distribution of Rents for Public Assistance
and Other Tenants, New York City, 1978*

Rent (S)	Public Assistance Tenants		Nonpublic Assistance Tenants	
	Number (in 000's)	Percent	Number (in 000's)	Percent
Less than $100	21.0	8.7	149	9.3
100–124	17.0	7.2	136	8.5
125–149	55.0	22.9	179	11.2
150–199	85.0	35.3	401	25.0
200–249	44.0	18.2	303	18.9
250–299	13.0	5.4	182	11.4
300–399	4.0	1.7	146	9.1
400–499	0.7	0.3	54	3.4
500 or more	0.6	0.2	52	3.2
Unreported	1.7		85	
Total	242.0	100.0	1688	100.0
Median	$165.56		$191.16	

Source: U.S. Bureau of Census

so much by a family deciding to become destructive, as in its having little incentive to curb its normal spontaneous behavior.) It can complain of code violations, with or without justification (or of its own creation). It may also have a legitimate reason to move in the event of the abandonment or destruction by fire of its buildings, although it is frequently alleged that a sizable number of welfare families commit arson themselves in order to qualify to move.

There is evidence that the tightened restrictions regarding welfare tenant moves have not actually curtailed the rate of mobility.

The Tenants of Last Resort

What of the nonwelfare families in the areas experiencing intensive welfare occupancy, or about to experience it? A number of factors make it impossible for welfare and nonwelfare families to coexist for very long, regardless of race. The most obvious reason is class. One of the imperatives of the housing market that must be recognized, or ignored by housing policy analysts at their peril, is the spatial self-segregation of families by social class. Given the importance of housing location as a status symbol, the qualitative differentiation of the bundle of public and private services and amenities that varies with neighborhood social status, the incongruity of social values among families of diverse socioeconomic classes, and above all, the fear of violence at the hands of poorer youths, very few families, whatever their ethnic or racial background, will remain resident among families of a lower socioeconomic status than their own. Welfare families are perceived almost universally, as ipso facto occupying the lowest rung on the socioeconomic ladder.

By itself this would seem to assure that few nonwelfare families would remain in, or move to, areas of heavy welfare occupancy. This natural tendency gains considerable reinforcement from some additional factors unique to New York City. One of these is rent regulation. Although the impact of rent regulation in the New York City housing market will be discussed in Chapter IV in greater detail, at this time it need only be pointed out that the city's rent regulations permit significant rent increases only when an apartment turns over. Welfare families, as discussed earlier, are a great deal more mobile than the rest of the population. Therefore, apartments vacated by welfare tenants can have their rents set above those prevailing in rent controlled apartments occupied by nonwelfare tenants, and perhaps even above levels dictated by the underlying housing market. Given the typical landlord's resentment of rent control, few landlords miss the opportunity to raise rents upon vacancy. This assures that even the least snobbish or least fearful nonwelfare family will pass up vacant apartments in welfare occupied buildings as long as they appear to be more expensive than controlled apartments of the same quality.

Even if this did not make welfare families the tenants of last resort, DSS shelter allowance schedules are often more generous (especially in the case of large families) than either rent regulations or the underlying market. Taken together, then, the natural forces of socioeconomic segregation are reinforced by the overpricing of welfare tenanted apartments, and further reinforced by the subsidization of welfare families, assuring that once buildings contain a significant proportion of welfare tenants they will become all welfare, and by extension districts comprised of many welfare buildings will become welfare neighborhoods.

This generalization may seem to be neither novel nor surprising. Its significance lies only in the context of the dynamic described above that assures the constant mobility of the city's welfare population. If the nature of New York's shelter allowance program (operating in concert with slack housing demand, the behavior of the adjudicatory system, rent regulation, etc.) keeps welfare families on the move, and if other families (regardless of race) keep avoiding them, we have set in motion a process that must create a continuing demand vacuum and one that can only result in abandonment. Ahead of the welfare wave, non-welfare families flee (or are not replaced) creating a vacuum to be filled by the advancing tide of welfare families. Behind the welfare wave there is a vacuum that no families will fill. In neither location is nonpathological retirement of the housing stock a remote possibility. In the areas undergoing the transition from nonwelfare to welfare any new increment of real estate investment is economically unattractive. The zone of abandonment, on the other hand, contains too many vestiges of poverty and deterioration, and in any case is much too far removed from the central business district or middle class residential neighborhoods, to justify redevelopment.

Table 8

Apartment House Tax Arrears and Welfare Dependency by Borough, New York City, 1978

Borough	Cumulative Tax Arrears		Welfare Dependency	
	Thousands of Dollars	Percent of Assessed Value	Number of Persons	Percent of Population
Manhattan	64,224	13.5	127,282	8.9
Bronx	64,577	54.4	216,025	15.6
Brooklyn	47,237	23.7	306,177	12.7
Queens	7,224	3.5	89,277	4.7
Richmond	691	7.1	13,077	3.3
New York City	183,953	21.0	751,838	10.0

Sources: NYC Finance Administration
NYC Department of Social Services

It must be emphasized at this point that we are confronting a phenomenon that varies from, and transcends in its impact on housing demand, the normal dynamic of simple neighborhood racial change described earlier. For one thing, New York's welfare population and its minority population are not one and the same. As of 1978 the city contained 408,000 non-Puerto Rican black families, and 228,000 Puerto Rican (birth or background) families, with only 97,000 of the former and 90,000 of the latter receiving public assistance. In other words, 449,000 minority families in New York City are not on welfare. Many of these families are often caught up in the throes of neighborhood destruction, but they are as determined to evade its consequences as white families, and they do not contribute significantly to the ecology of destruction, except insofar as racism softens the housing market in areas of recent minority settlement and raises the vacancy rate somewhat.

More significantly, even rapid racial change in sections of a city should eventually result in a new equilibrium and a reasonable stability of tenure. The modified filtering model described earlier would predict some potential abandonment in the most deteriorated sections of the ghettos left behind, and some in a zone of transition that demarcates the boundary between the outer perimeter of potential racial change and the predominantly white areas beyond it. However, the dynamic of wholesale racial turnover should be self-limiting. If there are significant disparities between the quality of housing in the expanded ghetto and the white neighborhoods beyond its furthest boundary that might spur minority group mobility, these should be reflected in price differentials that would exclude all but the most affluent minority families. If there are no significant disparities in housing quality, minority families will have little incentive to move unless the aggregate minority population was growing. In that case, however, there should be low vacancy rates in both the original ghetto and the transitional areas, making both areas economically viable. Given the normal operation of market forces, even in cities with large minority populations where all families, regardless of race, carefully weigh the value of better housing as against other discretionary consumer expenditures, and landlords ask for and get fair market rents that reflect the amenity level of their housing units, we should expect rapid neighborhood racial change and abandonment levels consistent with the net decline in the city's population, but not a perpetually moving avalanche of devastation.

The hypothesis that the ecology of housing destruction is linked far more strongly to the mobility of welfare families than to racial change per se can be supported by comparing the rates of tax delinquency in minority dominated neighborhoods with a small percentage of public assistance families with those where welfare tenancy is pervasive.

Table 9

Analysis of All Minority-Dominated Census Tracts in Terms of Welfare Dependency and Incipient Abandonment, New York City

Variables	Coefficient of Correlation
All Tracts:	
TAX/MIN	.3342
TAX/WEL	.4059
Excluding Manhattan:	
TAX/MIN	.2839
TAX/WEL	.5064

Variables

MIN: *Minority Dominance*-black and Hispanic population as percentage of tract total

WEL: *Welfare Dependence*-welfare recipients as percentage of tract population

TAX: *Tax Arrearage* -percentage of tract parcels in tax arrears for more than five quarters

Source: Author's analysis of data furnished by NYC Department of City Planning

Table 9 displays the results of an analysis of all minority-dominated census tracts in New York City with respect to degrees of welfare dependency and incipient abandonment (as indicated by long-term tax delinquency). Although the degree of correlation of tax arrearage with minority occupancy is not insignificant, the correlation with welfare dependency is much greater, especially when Manhattan is excluded from consideration, and strongly documents the link between welfare dependency and abandonment, independent of racial factors.

Summary

To summarize the contribution of the public assistance system to the ecology of housing destruction, welfare families are entitled to discrete, unfungible shelter allowances that:

a. permit them to penetrate middle class neighborhoods where rent regulation has kept rents at levels within the shelter allowance guidelines and rising vacancy rates make welfare families acceptable to anxious landlords;

b. tempt them to withhold their allowances from their landlords and spend them because there are no meaningful sanctions applied by the department of social services or anyone else against rent delinquent tenants, making buildings with a large number of such tenants uneconomic;

c. encourage their constant mobility, either because rent delinquency must result in eventual eviction or building abandonment; or because a constant or rising maximum shelter allowance (the al-

lowance will increase if the family size increases),
in a housing market where there are always better
apartments available beyond the zone of deterioration, will entice many welfare families to use
their shelter allowance to the limit and obtain the
best housing available;

d. discourage nonwelfare families from remaining in,
or moving to, the areas of high welfare tenancy
because, given prejudices and fears (crime, noise,
status, etc.) in a city of rent regulated apartments
that are often cheap even in good neighborhoods,
deteriorated apartments whose rents coincide with
the shelter allowance schedule will seem overpriced;

e. encourage landlords in areas not yet significantly
impacted to accept welfare families either because
of the collapse of nonwelfare demand in anticipation of impending change, or because shelter allowance guidelines may exceed former controlled
and even market rents, a phenomenon that gains
significant force as ever more welfare families are
issued "two-party" (tenant-landlord) checks.

NOTES

1. New York State Department of Audit and Control, Office of Welfare Inspector General, *An Examination of Rental Payments Made
   to Private Landlords by New York City Public Assistance Recipients*, February 1977, p. 11.
2. Conversation with Deputy Commissioner Martin Burdick, New
   York City Human Resources Administration.
3. N.Y.S. Department of Audit and Control, *An Examination of
   Rental Payments*, p. 8.
4. Ibid., p. 12.
5. New York State Department of Social Services, Application to U.S.

HEW for "A Demonstration in the Use of AFDC Two-Party Rent Checks to Encourage Housing Repairs and to Aid Neighborhood Stabilization," 13 December 1978, and response to U.S. HEW Commissioner B.L. VanLare by N.Y.S. Commissioner B.B. Blum, 25 January 1979.

CHAPTER IV

RENT REGULATION

New York City's longstanding and pervasive system of rent regulation is often blamed for the dynamics of housing abandonment.[1] The argument is simple. A typical landlord's costs of financing, maintenance, taxes and utilities cannot be met by a rent roll depressed at arbitrarily low levels by regulated rents. A landlord caught in a "rent gap" squeeze must, perforce, abandon his building in the face of negative economic returns.

There are several problems with this thesis. For one thing, virtually the entire rental stock of the city is under rent regulation, while only certain neighborhoods experience a significant degree of landlord abandonment. In fact many regulated buildings exist in good repair in the very best neighborhoods of the city. For another, many of the buildings that have been abandoned, or are about to be, have benefited by a reduction in the severity of rent regulation to a greater degree than the rest of the stock.

These anomalous conditions can be explained easily by observing that rent regulation in New York City, like any other factor that depresses the rate of return (e.g., high taxes, restrictive zoning, etc.) has been capitalized in the value of the housing stock. Accepting the probability that most of the city's rental buildings have been acquired since rent regulations were first imposed (1943), we can assume that the acquisition prices of most buildings have accurately reflected their rate of return. What of changing circumstances, such as rising taxes, fuel prices and higher finance changes that may have changed a building's economic viability since its purchase? In New York's rental real estate market, buildings have turned over often enough to reflect such changing circumstances, and future adverse economic conditions are more than anticipated in large acquisition price discounts.

However, it can be argued that rent regulation in New York City has contributed substantially to the ecology of housing destruction, even if it has not done so by creating a "rent gap." Its contribution has been manifested in the creation of the following conditions in the city's housing market. By keeping rents, even in the more desirable neighborhoods, arbitrarily low, rent regulation has permitted the widespread infiltration of public assistance families into middle class neighborhoods. As noted earlier, given the prevailing schedules of shelter allowances (Table 6), market rents would have excluded welfare families from many areas now absorbed in the zone of destruction. By chronically depressing building prices through the capitalization effect, rent regulation has permitted the value of many structures to fall below the cost of satisfying tax and mortgage liens, or perhaps even the cost of normal maintenance increments (e.g., a new boiler). As Chapter VI will detail, this phenomenon, much more than the "rent gap," encourages some owners to walk away from their buildings, and others to sell their properties to a class of less experienced or more exploitative landlords.

Perhaps as important as the foregoing factors, rent regulation has subjected virtually every rental structure in the city to the detailed and continuous scrutiny of the public sector, with a number of adverse consequences. The most damaging of these (from the point of view of maintaining the economic viability of the housing stock) has been the tendency of the public sector to link the degree of severity of rent regulation, and relief from rent delinquency, to purported levels of building maintenance or amenity. In other words, the rent regulation system has created a set of building dossiers which permit landlords to be "punished" in a variety of ways for "bad behavior." For marginal landlords such "punishment" creates only one more incentive to relinquish building ownership.

Thus, rent regulation is at the crossroads of the ecology of housing destruction. It is the handmaiden of welfare housing allowances in encouraging welfare population mobility. It is the lubricant in the marginal real estate market that encourages landlord mobility. And it is an accomplice of the landlord-tenant adjudicatory process, and an agent in its own right, in making anything but the most limited real estate investment hazardous in all areas of the city where housing demand is currently or potentially weak. It has contributed all of this, over and above its probable role in depressing the level of investment in the construction of new housing and the maintenance of the old, over a period of nearly four decades.

A Legacy of Market Distortion

The system of rent regulation in force today in New York City is unequalled anywhere in the country in its complexity, and represents a truly remarkable accomplishment in legislative and bureaucratic improvisation. It has also proven to be remarkably durable and politically unassailable in its nearly four decades of life. Precisely because of recently legislated increments of complexity the common usage of "rent control" has been eschewed in favor of the broader and more general term of rent regulation.

Rent controls, in the conventional sense, were adopted by the federal government in 1943 as a wartime emergency measure to protect all tenants from rent gouging during a period of continuing housing shortages. When the national emergency legislation lapsed after the war ended, New York City and New York State elected to continue controls. As it applied to the housing stock of New York City, the legislation protected tenants in apartment buildings built before 1948 from any rent increases except those justified by capital improvements installed with the permission of the tenant and a 15 per cent increase attendant upon each turnover of occupancy.

In 1962 the state ended rent control for New York City but the city elected to keep the system within its jurisdiction as long as the citywide housing vacancy rate fell below 5 percent. Not unexpectedly the vacancy rate never rose above the trigger threshold and controls remained in force, with only minor modifications until the first significant recasting of the law in 1970. Some adjustments were adopted over the years. For example, in 1953 (during the Korean War) all controlled units were allowed a 15 percent increase; in 1957 small, expensive "luxury" apartments were decontrolled; and the 1962 legislation permitted apartments in small owner-occupied buildings with under six units to be decontrolled. Rent control continued as a way of life in the housing market of the city over these three decades, and it was generally accepted. For a considerable portion of this period prices nationwide were relatively stable, and as has been indicated earlier, any depressing effects that rent control may have had on building rent rolls were capitalized in building prices.

As any economist would expect, and as many have pointed out, there have been significant market distortions. The vacancy rate never rose because the artificially low rents under controls kept housing demand high. This higher than normal demand was manifested primarily in the overconsumption of housing space by households who found it economically viable to maintain nominal occupancy of larger apartments than they needed, or often ones that they did not need at all.[2] Because only the pre-1948 stock fell under controls, it was hard for newer apartments to be competitive in rents with the controlled stock. They had two attendant consequences. First, housing developers were willing to put up unsubsidized rental structures only in areas of very robust demand, such as the high rent districts of Manhattan and Queens, the southern part of Brooklyn, and Riverdale in the Bronx. Second, a very vigorous black market in controlled apartments resulted. Only with a bribe to someone, be it a former tenant (in the form of "key money," or buying the former tenant's furniture), the doorman, the superintendent, the building owner or any combination of these could one gain occupancy of a rent controlled unit.

Two market distortions are especially pertinent to the ecology of housing destruction. Although there is evidence that indicates that many owners of rent controlled structures were not unduly harmed economically by rent control per se, this was so primarily because owners stinted severely on maintenance. This was true especially with respect to the more expensive hidden maintenance items: heating, electrical and plumbing systems, major structural repairs, elevators, etc., with limited maintenance budgets devoted primarily to cosmetic items. As a result, many apparently sound and attractive structures embody large and fundamental maintenance "debts" that must be repaid if the structures are to survive in reasonable condition.

The other relevant distortion has been alluded to previously in a number of contexts. By depressing rent below market levels, rent control premitted the infiltration of poorer families, especially those on welfare armed with shelter allowance checks, into stable middle class neighborhoods. This assertion must be qualified, however. In the really desirable neighborhoods of the city, something approaching class based housing allocations prevailed, even in the face of rent control, through the operation of the black market and an informal network of information and references. The neighborhoods where controlled apartments could be secured without a bribe or premium were already becoming marginal in terms of their desirability. This was manifested in vacancy rates high enough for landlords to risk renting to low income or welfare families in the face of slack demand among their traditional clientele.

Nonetheless, in the absence of rent control, market rents might have remained high enough to maintain a middle or lower middle class tenantry, even as a certain amount of downward filtering took place. This is an assertion that is hard to document, but it gains support from the idiosyncratic geographical incidence of housing destruction. Where the penetration of welfare families has not been evident, for one reason or another, neighborhoods comprised of a large stock of controlled housing have been able to sustain their attractiveness to a predominantly middle or lower middle class clientele. In other words, controlled rents may have been a necessary, but not sufficient, condition for the operation of the ecology of housing destruction.

Economically based residential segregation and inferior

housing conditions are, of course, antithetical to most architects of housing policy. Nor, in the abstract, are they very acceptable to the population at large. Accordingly, rent control has been justified, over the years, precisely because it was supposed to be beneficial to the poor.[3] It was argued that under rent control all families in controlled buildings could afford better apartments than they would be able to under market conditions, and for poorer families in particular, rent controls provided the margin to enable them to occupy decent rather than slum housing.

This argument can be refuted on a number of grounds. By discouraging the replacement of older tenement housing with new unsubsidized structures in all but the best neighborhoods, rent control may have contributed to a lowering of the quality of the city housing stock in the aggregate. New York City does not compare especially favorably with other American cities in the general quality of its housing, probably for this reason. Second, by causing landlords to defer building maintenance, the imputed gains of rent control from the point of view of the tenant have actually been cancelled by a reduction of apartment or structure quality. And where apartments and structures have remained desirable, the economic benefits of rent control have often been discounted in the payment of black market premiums to acquire controlled apartments. Even the welfare and other lower income families that have penetrated otherwise out-of-reach precincts with the help of controlled rents have not benefited for long. Just as they appear to profit from the filtering experience, their new neighborhoods deteriorate around them.

In any case, for most of the rent control era, until 1970, most poor families lived in old and new law tenements, which might not have commanded market rents much higher than controlled ones. The real beneficiaries, as has been well documented, have been those middle class families occupying apartments, buildings and neighborhoods where the disparity between market and controlled rents have been much greater. Unquestionably, the durability of controls can be largely attributed to their popularity not among the poor, but with the mainstream middle class voters of the city.

Recent Modifications

A number of important changes took place in New York City's system of rent regulation between 1969 and 1974. Several studies commissioned by the city to examine the causes for the continuing deterioration of its housing stock, with particular attention directed to the contribution of rent control, provided the conceptual foundation for two changes in the implementation of rent control, both aimed at greatly reducing its negative economic impact on building owners.[4] Perversely, at approximately the same time, a large proportion of the remaining housing stock was suddenly brought under another form of rent regulation.

The more complex of the changes in rent control was the introduction of the maximum base rent (MBR) system legislated into being in 1970. Clearly a child of the "rent gap" theory of housing deterioration and abandonment, the MBR program was directed at insuring an owner a fair rate of return on his property. MBR entitles owners of rent controlled units to 7½ percent annual rent increases on all their apartments until a "maximum base rent" ceiling is reached. The maximum base rent for each apartment is based on its ideal pro rata contribution to the income of its building, such that the building's aggregate rent roll is sufficient to cover all owner expenses plus a competitive rate of return, set somewhat arbitrarily (and unrealistically) at eight percent.

The difficulties of implementing, monitoring and conforming with such a program have proven to be staggering. Detailed information must be secured and stored on every one of the 1,265,000 originally rent controlled apartments of the city, including presumably accurate information on idiosyncratic aspects of each building's operating costs. The MBR program also qualified rent increase entitlements by making all apartments with code violations ineligible, necessitating the cross-filing of an additional data set to keep track of each apartment's and building's condition. The program has proven to be an administrative nightmare for the city, and a very mixed blessing for landlords.

Reasonably full implementation of the MBR program was not achieved until 1975, five years after its legislative birth. Landlords have complained bitterly of the paperwork entailed in applying for MBR program rent increases, and the impossibility of meeting building code standards (which can be concerned with very minor qualitative deficiencies), under circumstances where irresponsible or rent-increase-evading tenants are able to undermine a building's record of code compliance. Both problems afflict disproportionately the owners of smaller structures in marginal neighborhoods, because the large scale owners of prime real estate are generally far better equipped to handle massive paperwork and code complaints. Thus, the very sector presumably most afflicted by "rent gap" economics, has been least able to take advantage of the MBR reform. As of 1979 fully one third of all rent controlled apartments did not qualify for rent increases under the MBR system. Nevertheless, MBR has taken hold, and some of the most egregious disparities between market and controlled rents have been reduced since the implementation of MBR.

Shortly after the MBR program was launched, the New York State legislature passed a vacancy decontrol law in 1971. The intent of this legislation was to phase New York City out of rent control altogether by removing from the constraint of rent regulation all vacated apartments. To assure that controlled tenants would not be harassed into vacating their apartments prematurely, the law provided for fines and other sanctions to be applied against owners found guilty of such practices. Since the documentation of vacancy is a lot easier than the documentation of building expenses and code compliance, and since there was originally no ceiling on post-decontrol rents, the vacancy decontrol reform was a great deal more helpful to owners than MBR, too helpful, as it turned out. But an account of the ultimate fate of vacancy decontrol awaits the description of an entirely different rent regulation development of this period.

The real estate boom of the early 1960's, precipitated by anticipatory development designed to evade the stricter new zoning ordinance of 1961 was followed by a virtual cessation of new housing construction. The sudden dearth of apartments in the late 1960's, at a time of a short lived economic resurgence in the city (a growth in city jobs, for example, from 3.4. million in 1958 to 3.8 million in 1969) brought about a succession of unusually high rent increases in the uncontrolled stock. To have to pay market, rather than controlled, rents is victimization enough; to endure large lease renewal rent increases is intolerable. In this spirit the uncontrolled tenantry of the city demanded relief. Eschewing the option of placing the remaining rental stock under the existing rent control system, the city in 1969 legislated a new quasi-public program of rent regulation to cover the bulk of these units.

Called "rent stabilization," the program provided for varying annual rent increase ceilings, to be applied across-the-board, and to be implemented and administered by the ownership sector itself. The legislation provided for a Rent Stabilization Association (RSA) to be comprised of all owners of uncontrolled apartments in structures of six apartments or more, with a voice in the organization in proportion to their holdings. The association is charged with the task of registering all owners in the program and levying an annual tax upon them to meet the operating costs of the rent stabilization system. The nine member Rent Guidelines Board, appointed by the mayor, each year sets new and renewal lease increases for the next twelve month period. Typically the guidelines specify permissible percentage increases for one year, two year and three years leases under conditions of either continuous or new tenancy.

Table 10 indicates the schedule of rent guidelines since the inception of the program. By law the annual guidelines must reflect changes in building operating costs and all other relevant economic factors involved in the operation and financing of rental housing. Unlike the MBR program there is no attempt to account for individual building idiosyncrasies in the guidelines. To deal with aspects of guideline levels that fail to reflect the problems of specific owners, and to handle such tenant rent increase and other complaints that arise, is a function of the nine member Conciliation and Appeals Board, also appointed by the mayor.

Even in this cursory description of the rent stabilization program, it is easy to discern its inevitable impact on rent levels in the affected stock. Depending upon each apartment's idiosyncratic history of one, two, or three year leases (the tenant has the option of specifying the term of his lease) and frequency of turnover, within a short period of time, apartments of identical or comparable market value prior to the program's implementation will vary widely in their rents. Thus rent stabilization immediately

Table 10

*Rent Increases in Percentage and Constant Dollar Terms
Under New York City Rent Stabilization Program
1972-1980*

For leases in effect between	Permissible percentage rent increases by term of lease			Effective constant dollar rents assuming $200 rent in 1972 by term of lease		
	1 yr.	2 yrs.	3 yrs.	1 yr.	2 yrs.	3 yrs.
7/1/72-6/30/73	4	6	8	196	200	203
7/1/73-6/30/74	4	6	8	184	181	184
7/1/74-6/30/75	6½	8½	10	182	182	171
7/1/75-6/30/76	6	7½	10½	182	171	278
7/1/76-6/30/77	4½	5½	8	179	171	168
7/1/77-6/30/78	5½	7½	11	179	162	159
7/1/78-6/30/79	7	8½	9	176	162	160
7/1/79-6/30/80	8½	12	15	176	148	146

Source: N.Y.C. Rent Stabilization Association

introduced an additional note of arbitrariness in the city's apartment rent structure. Not only could the rents of controlled apartments vary capriciously from uncontrolled ones, rents in controlled apartments prior to MBR could vary depending on turnover, history of capital improvements, and their relative rents in 1943. Now the rents in the uncontrolled sector would soon bear little relationship to the discipline of the market. Other than the residual tendency, even without a black market, for the rent structure to manifest somewhat higher prices in the very best parts of the city, one might as well determine each apartment's rent by lottery.

The system of rent regulation did not, however, bloom to the full flower of its complexity until 1974, when the vacancy decontrol law was modified with passage of New York State's Emergency Tenant Protection Act. Tenant organizations and a temporary state legislative commission asserted that the passage of vacancy decontrol resulted in drastic rent increases in a not insignificant number of instances, especially in parts of the city where housing demand was strong. The response of the New York State legislature was to repeal unqualified vacancy decontrol and replace it with legislation that placed all vacated formerly controlled apartments under rent stabilization. During the transition from controlled to stabilized status each apartment would be entitled to a one time rent increase to bring it into conformity with prevailing market rents for similar (in terms of location, amenity, etc.) units. The effect of this new development in the history of New York City rent regulation was to shift 623,000 units from rent control to rent stabilization in the short space of five years from 1970 to 1975. Perhaps as important, an entirely new class of owners and tenants are now a party to the stabilization program. Where the original stabilization buildings comprised what is loosely referred to as "luxury apartment houses," now most of the stabilized stock involves small buildings in marginal neighborhoods. The Conciliation and Appeals Board is now severely overtaxed, as its offices are ever more frequently invoked; and the RSA itself has been "captured" by a coalition of small owners.

Following is a brief review of the various permutations and possibilities under this newly-elaborated system of rent regulation. Approximately 402,000 apartments (about 32 percent of the rental stock) are still controlled, with a variety of nonmarket rents depending on the success of their owners in qualifying for 7½ percent annual increases, their official MBR, and the number of 7½ percent increments that have already been absorbed. Another 552,000 (about 29 percent of the total) apartments have moved from controlled status to stabilized status since the passage of the 1974 legislation, with a new set of guideline rent increases superimposed on their turnover "market rents." These apartments coexist in structures with those still under rent control. An additional 320,000 post 1947 units (or about 17 percent) are stabilized without ever having been controlled (the "original" stabilized stock). Their rents vary from market levels according to the internal eccentricities of the tenure-dependent features of the rent guideline process. Because the stabilization law excludes apartments in structures with fewer than six units, approximately 368,000 (or 19 percent of the total apartments, most in two and three family homes, are not controlled at all. The repertoire of nonmarket determined rents is complete if we consider the 165,000 apartments of the New York City Housing Authority whose rents reflect federal, state and city guidelines, and the 166,000 apartments (more or less) that enjoy one or another level of shallow public (federal, state, city) subsidy.

NOTES

1. See Frank S. Kristof, "Rent Control Within the Rental Housing Parameters of 1975," The American Real Estate and Urban Economics Association Journal, Vol. 3, No. 3, Winter 1975, pp. 47-60, and New York Telephone, Environmental Analysis Division, Corporate Planning Department, Rent Control at the Grassroots, 5 March 1976.
2. See Ira S. Lowry, Joseph S. DeSalvo, and Barbara M. Woodfill, Rental Housing in New York City, The Demand for Shelter, The New York City Rand Institute, June 1971, pp. 95-100.
3. For a discussion of the persistence of this rationale and some criticism of it see: B. Bruce Briggs, "Rent Control Must Go," New York Times Magazine, 8 April 1976 and Frank S. Kristof, The Effect of Rent Control and Rent Stabilization in New York City,

New York City Temporary Commission on City Finances, June 1977.
4. The foundations for the MBR reform of rent control were laid by studies commissioned by the city, prepared by the New York City Rand Institute, McKinsey and Company, and the Rutgers University Center for Urban Policy Research.

CHAPTER V

THE ADJUDICATORY SYSTEM

During any given month in recent years, over 150,000 tenants, or 8 percent of New York City's renters, are delinquent in the payment of their rents. In the aggregate rent delinquency amounts to $450 million per year or 10 percent of the entire rent roll. Furthermore, probably 50 percent of the delinquent tenants are families that, while poor in conventional socioeconomic terms, nevertheless receive subsidies to cover the entire amount of their rent obligations.[1] The really astounding fact, however, is that most landlords find it inordinately difficult to evict their rent delinquent tenants; conversely, most rent delinquent tenants can enjoy their apartments for long periods without paying rent. This state of affairs, one of the key elements in the city's ecology of housing destruction, is a direct result of its curious system of adjudicating landlord-tenant disputes.

The most fundamental assumption embodied in the

tenant-landlord contract is that the tenant must pay the landlord rent; if he fails to do so, he must vacate his premises. It does not occur to most tenants in this country that nonpayment of rent is even temporarily an option, since it is assumed that such behavior will result in swift and summary eviction. There are other aspects of the tenant-landlord relationship that are less fundamental, but are nevertheless embodied in the lease or in the law. The landlord is expected to keep his building and all tenants' apartments in good repair (however that is defined by law). The tenant must behave responsibly and with a certain degree of decorum (however that is defined in the lease). Sanctions can be imposed by tenant or landlord for an infringement or violation of these secondary agreements, but they are harder to document and less speedily enforced. In these respects the landlord-tenant relationship resembles all other seller-buyer or lessor-lessee agreements where the basic precondition for the consummation of a transaction is the payment of an agreed upon price by one party to receive the goods or services offered by the other, with certain additional understandings existing (explicit or implicit) as to the quality of the merchandise or service being exchanged. The remedy, in most cases, for a breach of faith with respect to merchandise quality is an annulment of the transaction where the buyer/lessee gets a refund and the seller/lessor gets back his merchandise or ceases to perform his service. Under almost no circumstances is the remedy for an unsatisfied purchaser/lessee the continued enjoyment of the "flawed" good or service for free.

But the New York City rental housing market seems to be an exception. Under current New York City law and judicial practice, the continued enjoyment of apartment occupation without payment of rent, under certain circumstances, has become another basic tenant "right." Along with rent control, this is part of the city's general strategy of trying to shift the economic burden of providing standard housing at moderate cost to the private ownership sector.

Creation of the Housing Court

Unlike rent control, the landlord tenant adjudicatory system has become less favorable to landlords and more favorable to tenants over the years, especially in the most recent period. But like rent control, the system enjoyed a long period of relative stability and was only recently (1972) modified in significant respects. Before 1972, the landlord-tenant adjudicatory system spanned civil and criminal courts, and operated in a fashion typical of most American urban jurisdictions. Landlords with tenants who were rent delinquent, or who violated their lease agreements in other respects, could seek relief in civil court. If rent delinquency or other lease violations could be documented, the courts would authorize tenant eviction. Over time the city courts grew increasingly reluctant to evict poor tenants, especially in cases where they confronted "slum landlords" with buildings in obvious disrepair. Increasingly, the courts in such cases would authorize or condone rent "withholding," but usually under circumstances where the court would hold all withheld rent monies in escrow. Nevertheless, court sanctioned rent withholding was the exception rather than the rule, and until the mid-1960's most landlords did not find it inordinately difficult to dispossess rent delinquent or otherwise offending tenants.

Under the pre-1973 system, complaints regarding building disrepair normally involved actions entirely independent of landlord attempts to collect back rents. Tenants in civil court, or the city in criminal court, could sue landlords to make such repairs as were required under either the city's building code or tenant lease provisions. If code violations or unfulfilled leasehold obligations could be documented, the courts could force landlords to make the necessary improvements, fine them or, in extreme cases, impose short prison sentences. As one would expect, the adjudicatory system was not especially effective in insuring high standards of building maintenance or repair. Given the reluctance of all citizens, but especially poor ones, to enter litigation of any sort, and the ponderous ways of the city's housing bureaucracy, not very many complaints against landlords were lodged relative to the size of the housing stock and the number of probable violations. Furthermore, given the necessity of documenting violations and repairs through the housing inspection system, relief was a very time consuming affair.

The growing vocality of tenant rights groups in the 1960's, building on a long-standing public antipathy to "slum landlords," created a widespread public perception that landlord-tenant adjudication was asymmetrical. Landlords could evict delinquent tenants at will and had the legal resources to do so. Tenants would have to waste a great deal of time and money to get landlords to fix up their apartments, with problematical chances of success after long delays, at best. It was this perception of asymmetry in tenant-landlord relations that prompted the major reform of this adjudicatory system, the creation in 1972 (taking effect in 1973), of the New York City Housing Court.

The housing court was created as a branch of the civil court system (by the act of the New York State legislature) to, in effect, remove tenant-landlord cases from other branches of the civil court, as well as make unnecessary most criminal prosecution of landlords. All cases involving housing related complaints, whether tenant or landlord initiated, would first be disposed of in the housing court. The significant policy change embodied in the housing court idea was the mandate written into the legislation that specified that the housing court must "recommend or employ any and all of the remedies, programs and sanctions authorized by Federal, State or local laws for the *enforcement of housing standards, regardless of the relief originally sought by the plaintiff* (emphasis added)." In other words, the business of the court was to be primarily directed to ensuring proper building maintenance and code compliance. Since most plaintiffs in landlord-tenant cases are landlords and since the relief sought is generally payment of back rent, this mandate clearly authorizes the court to establish a linkage between the formerly independent issues of rent delinquency and code compliance and, furthermore, to place code compliance ahead of rent collection as a judicial priority.

Invitation to Rent Delinquency

The housing court system, then, virtually invites rent delinquency as a remedy for purported levels of inferior building upkeep. It appears that the invitation has been widely accepted. It also appears that the various parts of the housing court have also heeded their mandate with respect to placing code compliance as a higher priority than rent collection. At present, in the majority of cases where a landlord sues for back rent, tenant representations are routinely made that rent arrears are being incurred because of code violations. In the disposition of the majority of these cases the housing court parts have ordered building and apartment repairs as a precondition for the payment of back rent. Furthermore, in most of these cases there is no holding of rent monies in escrow by the court, as was the practice in landlord-tenant court cases before 1973; nor does the court necessarily authorize payment of all back rent even when the removal of code violations is documented. Common practice is to "negotiate" a settlement between tenant and landlord where only a portion of the back rent is paid, under the justification either that the landlord was not entitled to his full rent before the apartment was put in satisfactory condition, or that the tenant, being poor, is in no financial position to make the full restitution. It should be noted that, in a large proportion of these cases, the delinquency does not involve tenants' income out-of-pocket, but rather the spending for other purposes of a welfare shelter allowance.

The impact of this curious adjudicatory system on building income flows, and on building values in the marginal real estate market, is predictable and will be discussed later in further detail. In the context of the legislative intent behind the creation of the housing court, the more immediate question is: has it increased the level of code compliance? The answer, not surprisingly, is no. In 1966 (under the old system) there were 593,000 code violations outstanding. In 1972, on the eve of the introduction of the new system there were 934,400. As of 1975 there were 1,146,800. So for all of its success in reducing landlords' rental income, and encouraging widespread tenant rent delinquency, the housing court has not succeeded in increasing the level of city-wide code compliance.

Housing Court Operations

As would be expected of a system responding to litigation, most complaints are filed by landlords who have the financial and legal resources to initiate suits. In 1976, out of a total of about 64,000 new housing court cases, 63,000 or 98.6 percent of the cases were filed by landlords, only 662 or 1.0 percent by the city's Housing and Development Administration, and a minuscule 256 cases, or 0.4 percent,

Table 11

Housing Code Violations,
New York City, 1966–1975

Year	Violations Reported	Violations Removed	Backlog of Violations Outstanding
1966	777,800	467,400	592,900
1967	602,700	506,500	683,100
1968	458,000	391,300	742,300
1969	283,900	404,600	619,500
1970	351,600	328,700	698,200
1971	380,300	355,700	722,800
1972	476,900	265,300	934,400
1973	373,900	281,600	1,026,700
1974	469,200	416,600	1,066,900
1975	554,700	461,500	1,146,800

Source: New York City, Office of Code Enforcement

were filed by tenants. In a typical year approximately 80 percent of the cases involved alleged rent delinquency and 3 percent tenant nuisance. Where rent delinquency is charged (62 percent of the cases) the disposition hinges on purported repair or service violations, and 36 percent on disputes concerning the amount of rent owed.

These disputes can concern either provisions of the city's complex rent regulation laws or disagreements as to the amount of rent previously paid. Disputed rent and code violation cases are not mutually exclusive categories. In other words, some tenant representations can involve both charges of apartment disrepair and disagreement as to the rent actually due. The typical case is not settled in less than five months, and virtually no cases are settled in less than three months. The average case is adjourned (held over) twice before settlement. If the landlord plaintiff loses interest in pressing a suit (as, for example, when

Table 12

Distribution of Housing Court Cases by Detailed Characteristics, New York, 1975

Characteristic	Percentage of Cases
Initial complainant and complaint	
Landlord	
Nonpayment of rent	79.3
Tenant nuisance	9.3
Tenant: Service or repairs	0.4
New York City (HDA): Service or repairs	1.0
Principal point of law	
Documentation of rent payment	20.0
Amount of rent due	19.3
Existence of code violations	60.7
Severity of code violations	
Type A	53.5
Type B	37.2
Type C	7.0

Source: New York City Office of the Comptroller, *Performance Analysis of the New York City Housing Court*, 1977 (sample of cases)

he walks away from the building involved) the case can be adjourned, permanently unsettled, as typically happens in 18 percent of all cases.

Cases can be settled in a number of ways. A tenant can be evicted. A tenant can be made to pay all or part of his rent arrears either with or without documentation that the landlord made necessary (as determined by inspections) repairs. Or a landlord can be required to remedy outstanding documented code violations without receiving any rent arrears. In most cases the hearing officer (de facto "judge")

tries to negotiate a settlement that is mutually agreeable
to both partners or, failing that, one that seems "fair."

A Typical Case

A typical housing court case might look something like
this. A landlord sues in housing court to dispossess a tenant three months in rent arrears. After an interval that can
vary from several weeks to more than a month a hearing
date is scheduled. The case can be adjourned, unsettled at
the first hearing for a variety of reasons. The landlord has
no copy of the lease (a common practice in the marginal
real estate market). The tenant does not respond to sum-
mons or requests an adjournment. The landlord's attorney, or the tenant's attorney, arrives too late for the
appointed hearing time.

Should the hearing go forward, the question of building
or apartment condition is raised almost immediately, potentially in a number of ways. The tenant can indicate
apartment or building disrepair as the basis for his rent
delinquency. If the tenant has legal representation (usually
legal aid, or federally funded legal services), his attorney
will almost certainly raise the repair issue. Or the hearing
officer can bring in the building's condition on his own
initiative.

In the atmosphere of housing court, especially in the
parts hearing cases originating in the city's marginal neighborhoods, i.e., those in or near the zones of destruction,
there is an a priori assumption that the landlord is guilty
of under maintenance, neglect, and code violation. In any
event, where the condition question is raised, the case
must be adjourned until a building inspection is made or a
check of the city's computerized building files is consulted.

Independently of the condition issue, there may be a dispute as to the amount of rent actually due. If the landlord is not well armed with accurate records, or the tenant or his representative with rent receipts, this can also precipitate an adjournment.

Another hearing date is scheduled and the parties reconvene for another hearing. Presumably the facts are now at the disposal of the hearing officer, who finds that the tenant indeed owed a specified amount of back rent, but that the apartment and building contains, say, seventy-five code violations of varying degrees of severity. The hearing officer rules that the landlord is entitled to all or part of his back rent when the violations are corrected. He may now require that the tenant place all or part of the arrears in an escrow account. Often, however, the tenant is absent, without legal representation, and such a ruling has no force. The case is adjourned again for a period deemed long enough to complete the repairs and conduct another inspection. The next hearing date arrives and a number of alternative possibilities exist, all predicated on the assumption that the landlord has maintained an interest in the case and made his repairs. If the tenant has failed to respond for the duration of the case, a dispossess order may be issued. If the tenant has placed the rent arrears in escrow, the landlord is entitled to go through the laborious procedure of retrieving it from the City Finance Administration. Or where the tenant or his attorney has shown at least a semblance of good faith as a party to the suit, a partial repayment of back rent is negotiated.

By now anywhere from three to six months have elapsed. The landlord now has an accumulated arrearage amounting to what was owed when he filed the case and that which accumulated during its disposition. He also has had to spend some sums of money to make the required repairs and to retain legal counsel. He may also have spent a great deal of time. Under the best of circumstances he gets all his back rent minus approximately 5 percent of the amount which is absorbed in a variety of city fees attendant upon the escrow process, and minus all repair and legal costs. Very often, however, all he gets after all this time, expenditure, and loss of income is the right to evict the tenant. The tenant, incidentally, if on welfare, simply moves on to another apartment, armed with the DSS shelter allowance, to start the process all over again, if he so chooses.

Code Violations

Before drawing some fairly obvious conclusions as to the impact of this system on the housing stock in or near the city's zones of destruction, the code compliance issue must be addressed briefly. New York City's Housing Maintenance Code enumerates three classes of potential violations. The least egregious category, "class A," includes nonhazardous violations that must be corrected within ninety days of any official notification as to their certified existence. Class A violations might include such items as cracked plaster, a poor paint job, leaky faucets, inoperative light fixtures. An intermediate category, "class B," includes violations that are presumably potentially hazardous and must be corrected within thirty days of owner notification. Typical class B violations include broken plaster, torn flooring, low water pressure, and sidewalk cracks. The most serious violations fall in the "class C" category and are deemed to be immediately hazardous in nature. Such violations must be corrected within five days of owner notification and also carry a fine of twenty-five dollars per day per violation for every day past the notification limit. Inadequate heat, roof leaks, malfunctioning bathroom fixtures, and blocked fire exits are examples of class C violations.

As has been indicated, failure to correct violations is problematical for landlords these days not so much because of the likelihood of city initiated prosecution but because city and state law now inextricably links the correction of code violations with the rent regulatory system and the adjudication of rent delinquency suits. In other words, the documentation of uncorrected code violations is meant to impose significant economic costs on offending landlords not through such traditional judicial sanctions as fines or imprisonment, but by reducing their rental income.

The code enforcement issue is a classic one that comes up often in any discussion of housing policy and housing economics, and the "slum landlord" guilty of code violations is a familiar scapegoat in both the popular mind and in the official literature related to public housing policy and legislation. The conventional view of code enforcement has been, nonetheless, economically naive. As was indicated in the introductory chapter, the economics of the stable slum automatically assumed a low level of building maintenance. Therefore, under the jurisdiction of any rigorous building code, slum buildings were bound to contain many code violations. If such violations were to be corrected without making the property unprofitable, the landlord would have had to charge higher rents and, perforce, aim his housing at a more affluent market.

From the inception of fairly strict building codes in the beginning of this century, their enforcement in terms of publicly initiated prosecution has been haphazard and largely ineffective. This may be attributed partly to the difficulty and cost of documenting and prosecuting code violations on a significant scale. For the most part, however, lax enforcement of building codes reflected the realization that rigid code compliance must result in the displacement of poor families. The economically correct assumption was that poor families could only afford substandard shelter.

Substandard housing is rightly to be deplored, but the expectation that the private housing market could provide standard shelter at rents low enough for the poorest families, without subsidies, was an exercise in economic wishful thinking. On the other hand, landlords inclined to be exploitative, who could absorb the costs of adequate levels of maintenance and repair, should have been kept in check through competition in the housing market. Unsatisfied tenants could and would find apartments at competitive rents in better maintained buildings.

The economic arguments for condoning widespread nonconformity with building codes have been weakened over the years, from the perspective of both housing supply and demand. Such filtering of the housing stock as has occurred furnishes marginal landlords with a much higher quality stock than in the past, whose maintenance in standard condition should not prove to be an excessive economic burden. At the same time, a much smaller proportion of the population is so poor that it can only afford substandard housing, and that segment that is still very poor, in New York City at least, receives shelter allowances pegged at middle income rental levels. This kind of reasoning is the basis for the increasingly hard-nosed, anti-landlord view behind New York City and State efforts to force code compliance by linking it to landlords' rent rolls.

Nevertheless, the continuing high numbers of outstanding code violations and the increasing destruction of the housing stock should furnish persuasive evidence that these policies have failed, however attractive their logical foundation. They have failed because in orienting policy solely toward disciplining the stereotypical slum landlord, they have neglected the potential for abuse on the tenant's part.

Tenant abuses fall into two principal but related categories. The first is rent delinquency, motivated not so much by the condition of the tenant's apartment (whatever the objective conditions might be), but by the desire to spend the normal rent allocation on other goods and services. The second is the tendency of a great many tenants to create code violations themselves. Tenant created code violations may be merely the result of irresponsible behavior or may be cynically motivated by the desire to document landlord code noncompliance to justify rent withholding. Often a casual tenant attitude toward his apartment or building can represent a blend of these motivations. Charges made by landlord groups and real estate interests of tenant created code violations are often dismissed as self-serving and pandering to negative stereotypes of poor and minority families. Nevertheless, building department inspectors' reports yield ample evidence that, self-serving or not, landlords have a case in making these accusations because tenant created code violations represent a large proportion of the total.

Code violations are classified by degree of hazard, presumably to permit actions (sanctions, repairs, etc.) in proportion to the severity of any documented violations. Yet, in linking code enforcement to rent regulation or adjudicatory relief from rent delinquency, there is little opportunity to fit the system's response to the actual importance of the code violation items cited. In other words, even class A violations are "rent impairing," when a landlord applies for rent increases under the MBR program, or can furnish the basis for court sanctioned rent withholding. This is significant because class A violations are the easiest for tenants to create. Inspectors have noted in their reports seeing broken window panes with the manufacturer's stickers still affixed. Tenants can easily take a hammer to their door, or to the plaster. They can easily stop up their toilets or their sinks. The city's housing code provides for the eviction of tenants proven to be responsible for code violations; but such behavior is difficult to document, and almost never enforced.

Not all code violations that cannot be attributed to landlord negligence are necessarily tenant created, at least not in the usual meaning of tenant. Given the poor security in most apartment buildings in marginal neighborhoods, it is easy for nontenants to enter the premises and commit acts of vandalism, or steal components of the building infrastructure, especially parts of the mechanical or electrical system, for resale. The higher a building's vacancy rate, the greater the likelihood of such "exogenously" created code violations.

So the landlord, no innocent to be sure, is placed in a double bind by the rent-linked code compliance system. If he conscientiously maintains his building, setting aside a reasonable proportion of his potential rental income for upkeep and repairs, he might still encounter instances of rent delinquency. These might be grounded in legitimate grievances based on building problems for which neither landlord or tenant are at fault, or they might be based on tenant created violations. Either way, the operation of the rent regulatory system and the housing court will insure that the landlord suffers at least a temporary, and perhaps a permanent, loss of rental income. This makes it more difficult to set aside money for maintenance, with the result that the number of certifiable code violations will increase. It also increases landlord cynicism which quickly is factored into his economic calculation concerning the building's future, contributing directly to its eventual participation in the ecology of housing destruction.

Effects in Nonmarginal Neighborhoods

As has been indicated, the ecology of housing destruction in the city is geographically fairly specific. Yet the housing adjudicatory and rent regulation systems are city-wide. What are the effects of code compliance-rent level linkage in nonmarginal areas of the city?

The full destructive potential of code compliance linkage is severely constrained elsewhere in the city, wherever there is a middle class tenantry and a robust demand for apartments. It can be argued, even without making invidious class distinctions, that the middle class tenants in nonmarginal neighborhoods, having larger discretionary incomes at their disposal and often leading more organized lives, are less apt to pursue rent delinquency strategies, or contribute as frequently to the creation of code violations.

But the class of the tenantry is important not so much from the perspective of tenant behavior, as from the attitude of the agencies enforcing code compliance, and the operation of the housing market. Landlords in nonmarginal areas are not as apt to be stereotyped as "slum landlords," nor the tenants as apt to be viewed as "victims of exploitation." Thus, more frequently, there will be case dispositions favorable to landlords. Precisely because they are economically more viable, the buildings in better neighborhoods will be owned by larger real estate concerns that are much more apt to have the administrative and legal resources to cope with the formal requirements of the rent regulatory and adjudicatory systems. They will be able to furnish leases and receipts for repairs undertaken; they will be able to correctly fill out the myriad forms needed to apply for relief under a variety of rubrics; they will act more swiftly in pressing eviction; and they may even have access to political influence at the top of the various agencies whom they must confront.

Behind all of these factors, of course, lies the strong demand for apartments in areas far from the zones of destruction. As much as middle class mores, a generic fear of displacement will keep tenants in such areas from pressing a rent delinquency strategy. Strong demand creates an incentive for the more professional class of building owners to put up with the city's red tape and persist in "beating the system." Strong demand also permits rent levels high enough, even under the constraints of rent regulation, to absorb high levels of maintenance.

To summarize, then, the landlord-tenant adjudicatory system, by inviting or condoning rent delinquency, insures that in marginal neighborhoods (those in or near the zones of destruction):

   a. a large proportion of the building rent rolls become uncollectable,

   b. tenants have an incentive to create code violations or at least to take a casual attitude toward them when they are created by others,

   c. landlords must absorb significant losses of time and money, without effectively reducing the volume of code violations or improving the upkeep of apartments or buildings.

Where the system is relatively innocuous in its impact, in stable middle-class neighborhoods, it is not necessary. Where serious and numerous code violations exist, the system is clearly counterproductive, hastening rather than retarding the deterioration and destruction of the housing stock.

NOTES

1. The actual degree of rent delinquency and its incidence among various classes of tenants is difficult to document. The estimates cited are drawn from surveys conducted by the Rent Stabilization Association, bolstered by the judgement of its executive director, Frank S. Kristof.

CHAPTER VI

THE MARGINAL REAL ESTATE MARKET

A common misperception on the part of those viewing the abandonment and devastation in the city's zones of destruction is the belief that building ownership in these areas is always unprofitable and that all landlords are driven from their buildings because their costs exceed their rents. (Ironically, this view may be articulated by the same people that accuse the landlord class of rent gouging or flagrant undermaintenance of their buildings.) Even granting the probability that quite a few well-intentioned and unwitting slum landlords just one day found themselves in a zone of destruction, most of the present and future owners of this kind of property are there by choice, and are making money. It is the case in virtually all markets that one can make money in a declining market as well as a rising one. In the stock market one can buy with an expectation of appreciation or one can buy in order to sell short.

The economics of the city's marginal real estate market represents the equivalent of selling short in housing.

To make this point is not to condemn, but to observe that the market will impose its will. When circumstances (such as ill-conceived public intervention) create market distortions of one kind or another, markets have a way of retaliating by unleashing a host of unintended and un-wanted consequences. Previous chapters have outlined, in some detail, the various components of the ecology of housing destruction that have distorted housing demand patterns in many areas of the city. These demand distor-tions have not made it impossible to make money in the city housing market, even in its marginal housing market. They have only led housing entrepreneurs to make money in ways that involve the destruction of the housing stock or, more accurately put, to make money even as the stock awaits its inevitable demise.

The most significant difference between the economics of the marginal real estate market and a normal one is the virtual absence or severe depression of property asset value. In a sound real estate market there will be a not insignificant acquisition cost, whether or not this involves a large investment of cash; and there is almost always an expectation of a stable or rising resale value. Even in the exceptional cases where resale values in an area are declin-ing, in most normal real estate markets the remaining value will be great enough that owners will want to retain title to their holdings.

The absence or depression of asset value on the part of residential property in or near the city's zones of housing destruction creates the following distortions in property owner behavior, distortions, that is, from the norm that prevails where there is some appreciable asset or resale value. Property owners have little incentive to:

a. invest in the maintenance, repair, let alone improvement, of the property beyond what is required to obtain maximum or optimal rental income. Any investment beyond this level is wasted, for it cannot be recaptured on sale;

b. honor such obligations as tax and mortgage payments beyond the period necessary to obtain some predetermined optimal return on investment. The only sanctions that creditors can impose are to place liens on the property or to foreclose, and such sanctions have no economic force if the property is worth nothing to begin with;

c. screen the potential tenantry to weed out potentially destructive, irresponsible, or otherwise undesirable households; especially if such discrimination would result in an appreciable number of vacancies in a slack market. The only reason for landlords to be discriminating in the selection of tenants is to conserve or enhance the condition (both physical and reputational) of the property with an eye to eventual resale. With resale expectations diminished, this incentive is considerably dissipated.

All of these distortions in owner motivations and behavior add up to the same thing. Buildings that have no or little or declining asset value are destined and often programmed for abandonment (and, hence, ultimate destruction) from the moment that they are acquired.

That such properties are acquired at all in spite of their shortcomings as capital assets is due to their lucrative potential as income producers in the short run. The actual income value of any specific property, and the length of time that it remains profitable, depends on a complex economic calculation which will be addressed in some detail further on. But the significant point to be made is that however high yielding a property might be at the point of acquisition, the ecology of housing destruction insures that at some point in the not too distant future the income potential of the property will be exhausted. If there were any expectation of long run income producing viability, the capital value of the property would, of course, not be so severely depreciated.

This fact is generally understood, but the incorrect conclusion often drawn from it is that this represents a "self-fulfilling prophecy." The argument runs that if only owners had faith in the future of their properties they would behave accordingly (i.e., not act on their negative expectations as indicated) and the cycle of abandonment would never be allowed to begin. The fallacy in this view is the assumption that the ownership sector's negative expectations do not represent an economically accurate response to the dynamics of the ecology of housing destruction outlined earlier. Thus, attempts to remedy the "self-fulfilling prophecy" without any attendant changes elsewhere in the housing market and housing systems (the market plus the various modalities of public intervention) are bound to fail, at least in the long run. In this area, as in so many others, policy analysts fail to give the market (i.e., individual entrepreneurs in a competitive economic setting) credit for knowing what it is doing. Even if many positive expectations in the market represent an excess of optimism, most negative expectations are well founded. And when the underlying negative forces change in ways that would make the activities at issue more profitable, the market responds quickly enough.

The Marginal Purchaser's Calculation

The degree to which a property in or near the path of housing destruction is viewed as profitable and the duration of its profitability depends on the following variables factored into a complex economic calculation:

a. acquisition cost, especially initial cash outlay,
b. effective rental income, taking into account vacancy and delinquency rates,
c. upkeep costs, including heat, utilities, insurance and maintenance,
d. property taxes, to the extent to which they must actually be paid,
e. financing costs, also to the extent to which they must be paid.

In the normal residential real estate market the objective is to acquire and manage property such that the rental income exceeds upkeep, tax and financing expenses by a large enough margin to yield a rate of return on invested capital (in this case the cash outlay) competitive with other potential investments. Since upkeep expenses and taxes are more or less exogenously determined, and fixed at any given time, when property is offered for sale an economic calculation balancing rental income against operating costs to arrive at some predetermined yield will specify the maximum cash investment that any purchaser should offer and depending on the kind of financing available, the maximum feasible purchase price.

The calculation should reflect the true rental income after allowing for vacancies, and should also discount any projected increases in operating expenses or anticipate any projected increases in rental income. As has been indicated, in the normal residential real estate market, in neighborhoods expected to be stable for a considerable period, a fixed or increasing resale value for the property is assumed. Where there is expectation of a rapid appreciation in value, the rate of return on the initial outlay may be depressed in the calculation. Conversely, where there is expectation of a decline in resale value the rate of return may have to be correspondingly greater.

How does the marginal real estate market differ from this model? Remarkably enough, what does not differ significantly between marginal and viable residential properties is the nominal rental income per room, or the typical upkeep expenses. A comparison of a representative sample of marginal and viable properties in a wide array of locations within and beyond the zones of destruction indicates that, on the average, the rental income, per room, is only 30 percent greater in viable area buildings than in marginal ones. Upkeep costs among the two kinds of properties are virtually identical with maintenance and heating costs running slightly lower in viable buildings. Whatever economic edge these factors might confer on the viable buildings is almost entirely offset by their higher taxes. Expressing these factors as ratios, the nominal rental income to expense-plus-tax ratio for marginal properties is slightly under 2.0, and for other properties slightly greater than 2.0. These findings effectively refute some key aspects of the rent gap thesis, indicating that it is not depressed permissible rent levels or excessively high upkeep or tax burdens that economically endanger marginal properties.

What does vary significantly between properties in good and bad neighborhoods is the cost of acquiring and financing them. Drawing on data from the same sample of properties alluded to above, the full prices and the cash outlay of viable properties are generally four times, and the financing costs over three times as great as those for marginal ones. Certainly, assuming comparable expected rates of return, the slight difference in the rent/upkeep-plus-tax ratio cannot account for this.

Table 13

Rental Income, Acquisition Costs and Operating Expenses
Sample of Marginal and Viable Properties
New York City, 1979

| | Dollars Per Room | |
Item	Average for Marginal Properties	Average for Viable Properties
Rental income (max.)	566	723
Acquisition costs:		
Full price	1,214	4,419
Cash	301	1,114
General financing	110	302
Annual operating expenses		
Taxes	62	114
Heat and utilities	132	109
Insurance	22	21
Maintenance	84	82
Total operating expenses	300	326

Source: Author's analysis of NYC real estate data.

The explanation lies in the enormous difference between nominal and expected rental income levels in the two kinds of properties. Healthy buildings are probably estimated to experience an average or maximum vacancy rate of 5 percent. For marginal buildings an imputed rate of rental income loss can be derived that will yield the same rate of return as prevails elsewhere in the residential market. Assuming a normal vacancy rate expectation of 5 percent, and a normal yield on initial outlay of approximately 12 percent, the prevailing sales prices and cash requirements for marginal properties in our sample can be translated into an imputed income loss rate at time of purchase of over 28 percent. This income loss results from some combination of abnormally high vacancy levels and abnormally high rent delinquency. This is one kind of response of the real estate market to some of the forces described earlier that produce such high rates of vacancy and rent delinquency.

The imputed income loss concept does not, by itself, explain the entire process that terminates in housing destruction. It would be conceivable to have high but stable income loss rates which would be capitalized in the sale prices of marginal properties, but would not necessarily precipitate owner abandonment. To result in actual housing destruction, rather than a mere depression of real estate values, the process must be dynamic, causing ever rising vacancy and delinquency rates. The constant mobility of the zones of destruction and their tenant cohorts assumes that this will be the case in all neighborhoods lying in their path.

These rising vacancy and rent delinquency rates for all buildings located in areas threatened by housing destruction are what precipitate a variety of responses in the marginal real estate market that are clearly pathological from the point of view of healthy housing market dynamics, and what distinguishes the housing destruction in the last decade from the more familiar ecology of the stable slum. It is the interaction of the welfare shelter allowance system, rent control, and the adjudicatory system conspiring to constantly increase the rate of rental income loss combined with the pathological response of the real estate markets that constitute the ecology of housing destruction.

To understand the impact of a rising rental income loss on the economics of a marginal building, the implications of rapidly declining asset value and those components of owner expenses that can be successfully evaded need to be examined.

Graduated Disinvestment

When properties are located in a stable neighborhood whether affluent or not, and the various ingredients of the economic calculation require only marginal adjustments to yield a constant rate of return, the most appropriate owner management strategy is a conservative and responsible one: take good care of the property, choose tenants with discrimination, pay your taxes, pay your creditors, and above all, obey the law. This is not the most appropriate management strategy for owners of property set in rapidly deteriorating neighborhoods with rising vacancy and rent delinquency rates. Here the owner or a succession of owners must constantly shift management strategies, becoming increasingly exploitative of the property as the economic context deteriorates: cutting more corners, taking greater risks vis-a-vis the property, the tenants and the law, to maintain an economic rationale for continuing participation in the marginal residential market. It is not material whether or not an owner may have predicated his purchase on stable expectations and a conservative management strategy; when economic conditions affecting his property change, he must respond exploitatively, sell out, or lose his shirt. Most buildings that are eventually caught in a zone of destruction began as viable properties. The gradual encroachment of the wave of housing deterioration continuously changes the economic context, so that with each turnover in ownership, purchase is predicated increasingly on a risk-taking strategy of short-term rental income exploitation, and less on a conservative strategy of long-term asset value maintenance. This is a process of graduated disinvestment. The terminal stage of the process is permanent owner abandonment.

Graduated disinvestment involves the deliberate shedding of one or another owner responsibility vis-a-vis the property in order to reduce expenses, or increase rental income, in the full knowledge that this will significantly depreciate the value of the property or render it worthless. The responsibilities most easily shed in whole or in part are:

a. the payment of debt service, especially in the case of mortgages held by previous owners,
b. the payment of property taxes,
c. upkeep expenses not explicitly related to the sustenance of rental flows,
d. the careful selection of tenants.
e. obedience to the letter of the law, in a variety of situations.

It is very difficult, if not impossible, to obtain new bank financing for property purchased in or near the city's zones of destruction. This has been called "redlining" (whereby banks presumably maintain city maps on which lending areas of unacceptable risk are outlined in red) and has been vociferously deplored by public officials, community groups, and academic housing policy analysts. The degree to which banks "redline" or the accuracy with which they assess the risk of lending in specific parts of the city will not be analyzed here. Undoubtedly, the rapid rate of housing destruction in the last decade has made housing lenders gun-shy, and thus some "redlining" may be unjustified. On the other hand, bank portfolios are also bulging with bad loans and defaulted mortages on properties now in zones of destruction. For the most part, bankers, like the real estate community itself, are aware of what is happening in the city and are economically justified in not investing their depositors' funds in property soon to be destroyed. This does not mean, however, that all purchases of marginal properties involve all-cash transactions. Where banks will not lend, sellers will. In many cases the seller is a bank. A nearly universal feature of sellers' prospectuses is a description of the owner's financing terms. They vary considerably in their details, in terms of interest rates, repayment periods, degree of amortization, etc. They also vary considerably with respect to the cash down payment required. What all of these variations amount to is a calculation whereby the more marginal the property, the higher the proportion of cash to the nominal full price, the smaller the actual amount of the cash outlay, and the less likely that the mortgage will be self-amortizing (who wants to pay off the mortgage on a worthless property?). What also varies is the expectation on the part of both buyer and seller as to whether the debt service payments will actually be made. The more marginal the property, the more likely that both parties will realize that at some none too distant time in the future, debt service payments will cease.

The shedding of debt service burdens is one of the earliest of the marginal property owner's accommodations to rising vacancy or rent delinquency rates. The former owner of the property who holds the mortgage can, of course, foreclose. The present owner is willing to accept this risk because (a) by this time he has already recouped his initial cash investment, and (b) he assumes, correctly in most cases, that the former owners will not want the property back.

Many buildings are financed with "balloon" mortgages where the debt service payments cover interest only for a specified period, at which time the entire mortgage comes due. Owners of such buildings may be willing to assume the annual interest charge but have no intention of paying off or refinancing the mortgage when it matures. Should foreclosure occur, the building will be resold at an even lower price, with or without new, but substantially more modest, financing. At some point for every such building, foreclosure is no longer a realistic option.

The most conspicuous of the shed responsibilities, because it is so precisely documented and has attracted such widespread government and media attention, is the payment of property taxes. It is, of course, the failure of owners to pay property taxes that seals the fate of property in the zones of destruction, the penultimate step in each building's eventual demise. While debt obligations might be ignored by owners with impunity, the city will eventually foreclose on every permanently tax delinquent property. This does not mean, however, that purchasers of marginal residential real estate intend to pay their property taxes. The degree to which, and the length of time for which, property taxes will be paid is a delicate and critical part of the purchaser's economic calculation. The economically optimal strategy involves retaining ownership of the property as long as possible, while paying the city as little in taxes as possible, to the point where the rental income has fallen so low, or other expenses have risen so high, that the cost of paying any further taxes exceeds the economic benefits (in ongoing rents collected) of continued ownership.

A critical factor in this calculation is the extent of city tolerance of tax delinquency. Formally the period of grace before tax delinquency foreclosure (in rem) proceedings are begun is quite short, one year, reduced in 1978 from an earlier prevailing grace period of three years. In practice the city may drag its feet in initiating foreclosure, or be satisfied with a partial payment of back taxes. Skillful owners can play the tax delinquency game very successfully by buying a considerable period of time in which to collect rents while paying no or minimal taxes.

Not all marginal residential properties are tax delinquent, of course, but the payment of taxes does not necessarily spare a building from abandonment. Given a declining rent roll, the payment of property taxes simply puts such a building in the red that much sooner. Many tax delinquent buildings are resold both before and after tax foreclosure. In the event of a sale prior to city foreclosure, the payment of delinquent taxes is part or most of the acquisition price. When the city sells such property at auction, it often wipes the slate clean, forgiving all tax arrears. Otherwise, the city will generally be content with payment of back taxes as the sales price.

Only the most minimal maintenance and upkeep expenses will be incurred as marginal properties become more worthless. The economics of managing such property requires that any unnecessary infrastructure improvements of cosmetic items be avoided altogether. The only reason for assuming some minimal levels of maintenance and repair is to retain tenants in a weak market and to collect rents where the size of the rent roll is linked to code compliance and rent regulation. To make this explicit is not to provide a justification for the linkage. As in the case of the marginal properties that are not tax delinquent, the greater the outlay for maintenance and repair, especially if it is incurred to remedy tenant and vandal created problems, the sooner the building will cease to be economically viable and the sooner it will be abandoned and destroyed. Ironically, even with such a strategy of undermaintenance, the actual expenditures per room for marginal properties are not much lower than for other property because of diseconomies of scale.

One would expect that, except within certain limits,

heating and utility costs in the marginal residential sector would be hard to reduce without making tenants very unhappy. That is essentially true and, thus, heating and utility costs often represent the largest single annual outlay in marginal buildings. The only exception, a limited one as yet, can be found in buildings programmed for occupancy only during the warm months of the year. Under this strategy, a building is purchased in the spring, milked for its rental income through the autumn, and then abandoned. Because of the inexorability of heating and utility outlays in a period of rising energy prices, this is one of the factors that threatens the economic viability of even the most exploitatively managed marginal buildings.

A strategy of short-term rental income exploitation where the long-term resale value of a building is completely discounted, is bound to make owners indifferent to the nature of their tenancy. The only considerations to be weighed in evaluating prospective tenants are the rents they can be charged, and likelihood of their paying them. The implications of such an orientation have been discussed in detail in Chapter III. Eventually even a high probability of rent delinquency is discounted in tenant selection as owners became more concerned with maintaining occupancy and minimizing vacancy rates. As was indicated earlier, any public policy geared to guaranteeing the rents of the mobile poverty population, such as one which increases the proportion of restricted two-party shelter allowances for welfare tenants, simply feeds the tendency of marginal property owners to be irresponsible with respect to tenant selection without solving the underlying problem of rising vacancy rates.

Some Marginal Scenarios

Following are prospective management scenarios for two hypothetical buildings at different locations, one within and one slightly beyond one of the city's major zones of destruction.

Building A is situated just beyond the most devastated core of the South Bronx in a block where almost half of the other buildings have been abandoned. It is a run-down five story new law tenement walk-up building with twenty apartments and seventy-five rooms. Fifteen of its seventeen occupied units are tenanted by welfare households, none paying maximum shelter allowance rents. Five apartments are still rentcontrolled, but only one qualifies for the maximum base rent (MBR). All the others are rent stabilized. The building has just been purchased for $30,000: $10,000 cash and $20,000 in a seller's self-amortizing ten year mortgage at 8½ percent interest. Thus, the sales price comes to $400 per room and the cash a mere $133 per room. Annual operating expenses are also low. Taxes amount to $23 per room, as low as applies to practically any apartment house in the city. Normal heat, utility, insurance and maintenance expenses will not exceed $215 per room in the first year of ownership and debt service would cost $38 per room. Potential maximum rental income at full occupancy with no delinquency is $36,000 per year or $480 per room, so that even with the assumption of all operating expenses, including taxes and debt service, the building could yield a net annual profit of $15,000 or 150 percent on the initial cash investment. The caveat, of course, is that the maximum rental income cannot be realized. At the time of purchase the building has three vacant apartments (a vacancy rate of 15 percent) and four rent delinquent tenants (a delinquency rate of 24 percent). The former owner has three dispossess suits pending in the housing court which the new owner can pursue or drop. Effective rental income is only $23,400 yielding a first year profit of $2,700 or 27 percent on initial outlay. This is no mean rate of return, but the new owner realizes that both the vacancy and delinquency rates will continue to rise. Should there be only one more vacant apartment and one more delinquent tenant, the building will operate at a loss, even without considering the impact of rising heat, utility, and upkeep expenses.

So the new owner embarks on a strategy of maximum income exploitation and a very short ownership tenure. He will increase the effective rental income by filling two vacant apartment with very large welfare families paying the maximum DSS rents (even as two other apartments become vacant), and reduce the delinquency level by the equivalent of one apartment by collecting the rents himself rather than leaving this chore to his superintendent as the previous owner did. He will shed the entire debt service burden and make only token tax payments to retain title to the building for three years. He will undertake only the most minimal repairs, even at the risk of losing stature in housing court, and cut $2,000 per year from the previous owner's repair budget. He maintains the building's insurance policy in force, however. This strategy cannot succeed beyond three years because rental income will surely fall with increased vacancy and delinquency, and the city will not tolerate any further tax arrears. When he walks away from the building at the end of the third year, this strategy will have yielded the owner a net income, after accounting for all expenses actually incurred, of $34,500 on an initial outlay of $10,000, a compounded annual return on investment of over 50 percent. If the owner were completely unscrupulous he could increase this return substantially by paying an arsonist to torch the building upon abandonment, collecting $20,000 in insurance claims. Even if he eschews this option, the profitability of this real estate venture will have been substantial. The expenditure of time, energy, and anxiety will have been considerable, but the fact that this entrepreneur also owns more than a dozen other buildings in the same general neighborhood mitigates this in the realization of both monetary and psychic economies of scale.

Building B is a fairly new (1940) elevator building in a pleasant neighborhood fifty-three blocks north of building A and thirty-six blocks beyond the current edge of the Bronx's zone of destruction. The building has thirty-seven apartments and 127 rooms, with an occupancy rate of 92 percent (34 units). Thirteen apartments are still rent controlled, all qualifying for the maximum base rent and twenty-five are rent stabilized. The tenantry is 50 percent white, 35 percent Hispanic and 15 percent black. Only seven apartments (20 percent) are tenanted by welfare families. The building is attractive, in excellent condition, and in every respect would seem to be a first class residential property. For any viable neighborhood it should command a high price, but because of its location just beyond the zone of destruction it has been sold by a local savings bank for $200,000 ($1,575 per room) with a cash requirement of only $50,000 ($394 per room). These are absurdly low figures if we consider that a virtually identical building in a comparable but viable neighborhood of Queens or Brooklyn would sell for $5,000 per room, and the cheapest new building would cost at least $10,000 per room today. The building's low price certainly cannot be justified by its current income potential, because with a rental income of $62,500, after allowing for vacancies, and expenses including taxes and mortgage (a ten year balloon at 9½ percent interest) of $47,000, the building can net $15,400 per year profit. This represents a return of 31 percent on initial outlay, respectable by any comparative standard. Obviously the building's future income potential is being significantly discounted because of its location and the expectation that sooner or later it will be engulfed by the wave of devastation.

The building is purchased by an experienced real estate firm with over fifty properties in various parts of the Bronx. While eschewing a strategy of complete income exploitation, the firm expects to keep the building for no more than five or six years. In order to increase the building's rental income, the firm embarks on an aggressive campaign to fill its vacant apartments, using the services of several store front real estate agencies located in commercial areas as far away as twenty blocks to the south. For the first two years this policy is effective in lowering the vacancy rate, but as a consequence the welfare tenant percentage rises rapidly. By the fourth year the income loss due to rent delinquency reaches over 21 percent. In the fifth year the new owners face a rent strike organized because of declining standards of maintenance and the firm decides to sell. The firm is able to sell the building for $170,000 in a deal where it receives $20,000 cash and transfers the balloon mortgage to the new owner. The profitability of the building during this period can be seen in the following display:

Including the $20,000 proceeds from the sale, the aggregate return of $77,900 on an initial investment of $50,000 will represent a cumulative annual rate of 9.3 percent, not a killing but, considering that all tax and debt service obligations were met, a respectable venture in New York's real estate market.

At the point of sale, however, the building will have become so marginally profitable that the new owner will probably have to pursue a strategy of complete income exploitation, terminating in tax delinquency and default on debt service. Ironically, the final owner may yet wrest

Year after Purchase

Item	1	2	3	4	5
Expenses	$47,100	$48,700	$50,500	$51,900	$51,000
Rent/util.	13,500	14,700	16,000	17,100	17,500
Insur./maint.	8,600	9,000	9,500	9,800	8,500
Taxes/debt ser.	25,000	25,000	25,000	25,000	25,000
Welfare tenants (%)	20	35	47	52	65
Vacancy (%)	9	5	5	8	11
Rent delinquency (%)	0	5	11	16	21
Net rental income	$62,500	$64,300	$62,900	$59,800	$56,200
Annual profit	$15,400	15,600	12,400	7,900	6,200
Cumulative profit	15,400	31,400	43,800	51,700	57,900

greater income from the building than the responsible intermediate owner.

These examples actually understate the profitability of investment in the marginal real estate market because they fail to reflect the numerous tax advantages that can accrue to owners who can avail themselves not only of depreciation and other deductions to cancel any tax obligation on their income from these buildings, but probably show paper losses to offset other income. Even so, an investor must know what he is doing to prosper in this kind of market. A misjudgment at any point in the process of purchase and management: paying too much for the property initially, failure to exploit the full rental income potential, tardiness in pursing a strategy of disinvestment, can be costly. Furthermore, to prosper in this environment takes nerves of steel and a great deal of experience: dealing with a difficult tenantry, the housing court, the department of social services and numerous city and state agencies; facing rent strikes, subpoenas, and foreclosure notices; risking bodily injury, vandalism and theft. It is not an especially pleasant way to make a living. The principal point developed in these examples, however, is that sooner or later, both for slum properties in the midst of devastation or for higher quality structures seemingly beyond its reach, the ecology of housing destruction will work its will.

Moving On

Mobility is a central feature of the ecology of housing destruction. The process organizes a set of mutually reinforcing incentives for tenants to move, and it also creates incentives for landlords to move. Landlords are both pushed and pulled along, helping to fuel the process and catching up with its consequences. The push is obvious. As buildings lose any potential for further income exploitation, they are abandoned. There is also a significant pull, however, that may encourage owners to abandon or "sell" their structures before their full income potential has been realized.

The example of building B is illustrative. The expectation of future deterioration in the path of housing destruction offers the same kind of temptation to landlords as it does to tenants. Just as tenants can always find better apartments at comparable (or within shelter allowance guideline) rents a few blocks away from their present apartments, landlords can always find properties with a better income potential at bargain prices at the outer edge of the zone. Given constraints on the number of buildings any owner can manage, and the need to withdraw capital from older buildings to finance new acquisitions, owners will divest themselves of their less profitable buildings, even when they are still in the black, to acquire newer, cleaner, better tenanted buildings whose income potential can be exploited at an earlier and less troublesome stage of the cycle of destruction.

This suggests not only a mobile landlord class, but a hierarchy within it. The more respectable owners and firms with the capital to buy the better properties constitute the leading edge of exploitation, operating under generally responsible standards of building management. The more marginal entrepreneurs, often called "finishers," with little venture capital "mop up," wringing the last drop of income from these properties, and constitute the private owners of last resort. The distinction between these owner categories may often be blurred, as many firms may have portfolios of properties in various stages of the process, and as others try to graduate to less marginal properties as their assets grow.

Tax Delinquency—The End of the Line

Property tax delinquency is not only the surest indicator of the degree to which the ecology of housing destruction has taken hold; for the properties that manifest it, it is also unquestionably the preliminary stage to their imminent disappearance from the housing stock. The acting out of the tax delinquency rites of a terminally afflicted property involves, essentially, movement through a three phase pipeline. The initial phase involves the accumulation, for a specific property, of tax arrears. In many cases, especially for smaller residential properties, this may only represent a brief lapse due to temporary financial difficulties. In some cases it may be a graduated phenomenon, where some quarterly tax payments are made but others are missed, before all tax payments permanently cease. In these and other instances, owners may negotiate tax arrears repayment plans or assign the payment of back taxes to the next purchaser as a condition of a sales agreement.

Eventually, all chronically tax delinquent properties are foreclosed by the city under *in rem* proceedings, the second phase of the pipeline. A 1978 change in the law shortened the grace period before foreclosure on tax delinquent property from three years to one year, with dramatic effect as will be discussed further on. The *in rem* process itself can drag on for many months or several years, largely at the discretion of the city. At the end of the pipeline, in the third phase, there is outright city ownership of the foreclosed stock. The city can, upon ownership, resell the property and bring it back under private ownership, manage the property itself, or vacate it completely and raze it. In practice the city has done all three to varying degrees, and is constantly reappraising the "mix" of these strategies to pursue.

The extent of tax delinquency in the residential rental sector and, hence, subsequent city takeover of these properties is truly staggering. As of March, 1978, over 21 percent of the entire rental stock in the city, comprising approximately 280,000 apartments, was in tax arrears, not counting those properties already *in rem*, or taken over by the city. Of this total, the amount of permanently tax delinquent (i.e., abandoned) stock is suggested by the fact that 50 percent of these properties were in arrears for more than two years. It is estimated that if the city continues to foreclose on tax delinquent properties at the rate it has exhibited during 1978-1979, by October of 1980 the city will be the owner-landlord of over 236,000 apartments, assuming that it allows the entire stock it inherits to stand.[1]

As one would expect, the phenomenon of tax delinquency and city foreclosure is geographically coterminous with the manifestation of housing destruction and is therefore distributed very unevenly around the city. Nearly 30 percent of the residential rental properties of the Bronx (with approximately 80,000 apartments) are tax delinquent; while only 7 percent of Queens' (with 18,000 apartments) are so afflicted. Furthermore, less than 20 percent of Queens' tax delinquencies are long term, as compared to over a third of the Bronx's. As in other indices of housing pathology, Brooklyn and Manhattan represent intermediate cases, with Manhattan's troubled stock residing almost entirely north of Central Park. Although tax arrears data has not been analyzed at a finer level of geographic disaggregation, it is undoubtedly a very sensitive index of active and incipient housing destruction, especially when viewed in terms of length of delinquency, and the volume of properties at different stages of the arrears-foreclosure pipeline.

Apart from tax delinquency serving as an accurate barometer of housing pathology, the city tax foreclosure process itself is related to the ecology of housing destruction in a number of respects. For one thing, the degree of leniency or forbearance exhibited by the city is a critical factor in the economics of marginal properties. In the strategy of graduated disinvestment the viable life of a property is shortened directly in proportion to the degree to which the city moves aggressively on tax collection. When the city officially curtailed its grace period from three years to one, literally thousands of properties became immediately unprofitable. At the time that the new grace period took effect, approximately 15,000 of almost 25,000 tax delinquent properties were in arrears for more than a year, justifying immediate foreclosure proceedings. Even under the new law, however, the city has a great deal of latitude in its handling of tax delinquency. It can negotiate extended repayment plans for tax arrears. Anyone expecting that these plans will result in more than token tax collections is naive, but it is a way of legally extending the grace period. The city can drag its feet during the *in rem* process itself, postponing the day of actual takeover. On the other hand, the once prevalent practice, intended or not, of turning a blind eye to tax arrears is made more difficult today by the city's sophisticated data processing system and the ability of any number of outside observers to protest obvious or flagrant attempts by city officials to circumvent the law.

Increasingly, however, the city would like to circumvent this law and must, by now, seriously regret the implementation of the one year foreclosure requirement.[2] For it is in the act of taking title to hundreds of thousands of apartments that the private sector no longer wants, that the ecology of housing destruction finally, uncompromisingly, comes home to roost on the city government's doorstep. And as the city struggles with all of the management and financial problems that have plagued the private ownership sector, those housing economists and members of the real estate industry who have long deplored elements of the ecology of housing destruction that lie clearly within the public sector's purview such as rent regulation and the adjudicatory system, can only smile cynically as they see the city housing officials squirm when the shoe is suddenly placed on their (collective) foot. The irony in this is all the more poignant when one considers that the motive for shortening the grace period was to curtail the exploitation of marginal property by private owners.

The public sector's response to its rapidly expanding role as the city's premier slum landlord is instructive. To begin with, the city has pressed, so far successfully, for permission to use hundreds of millions of dollars in federal community development funds (intended for capital improvements in the city's infrastructure and public facilities) as a management subsidy. Beyond this unprecedented perquisite unavailable to the private sector, and notwithstanding the advantage of an automatic property tax exemption, the city's housing officials are demanding for its stock exemption from rent regulation, placement of all of its welfare tenants on restricted (two-party) shelter allowance checks, and permission to redeploy its tenantry to minimize the vacancy rate in its buildings. Even as the city learns the rigorous lessons of slum landlordship in the midst of housing destruction, it has not yet moved to extend any of these privileges to the private sector.

With all of the economic advantages that the city can arrogate to itself to ease the burden of unwanted housing ownership, the city will not be able to evade or retard the ultimate demise of the housing it inherits in tax foreclosure. The ecology of housing destruction with its moving wave of terminal tenants has made these structures obsolete. When the private sector walks away it means that the last increment of housing utility has been wrung from these properties. No one wants to own them, and even with a residual, largely rent delinquent tenantry, no one wants to live in them. The vacancy rate in city-owned buildings as of February, 1979, is 66 percent, and expected to rise to nearly 70 percent by October of 1980. All that remains in store for most of the city-owned stock is demolition, with or without arson as a preliminary. The cycle of housing destruction is thus complete.

NOTES

1. Data furnished by N.Y.C. Department of Housing, Preservation and Development to support its application to U.S. HUD for permission to use federal community development funds to manage the *in rem* stock.

2. For documentation of this report, see N.Y.C. Planning Commission, *Report on the Fifth Year Community Development Plan and Program,* April 1979. This view is also supported by interviews with NYC HPD officials (who wish to remain anonymous).

CHAPTER VII

STEMMING THE TIDE

Two hundred thousand apartments have been destroyed within a decade. Another two hundred thousand are about to be, or are already, owned by the city of New York, and thus are in the pipeline to imminent destruction. Half of one borough and large parts of two others present such a picture of destruction that for the entire nation, if not much of the world, these areas and the city that harbors them epitomize the collapse of urban civilization. The most afflicted of these precints, the South Bronx, is a virtual wasteland and has entered the media's vocabulary as a code term for terminal urban cancer. How is this possible, after five decades of concerted public effort at the amelioration of housing conditions and after the city, state and federal governments have poured over $10 billion into the city's housing stock, with most of this subsidy targeted for low and moderate income families and in the face of a public assistance program which, at a cost of over $500 million per year, picks up the entire rental tab, at levels near the citywide average for all rentals, for every eligible low income family in the city? This is not 1890, when Jacob Riis described, in *How The Other Half Lives*, a time of no housing subsidies, virtually no public assistance, no regulation of owners or rents. Yet, for all the overcrowding and noisome conditions of the city's slums of that era, one could seriously question whether today's poor are much better housed. However one analyzes it, explains it, describes it, or makes apologies for it, the ongoing destruction of the city's housing stock is a scandal.

The irony and the tragedy is that this scandal is in many ways the product of a basically benign and well-intentioned public sector and a highly regulated and circumscribed private one; a far cry from the laissez-faire indifference and unchecked landlord exploitation that prevailed in the past. Because public policies have responded to short term problems and political pressures with ad hoc improvisation, or have been predicated on poorly grounded and undocumented theories, they have served to exacerbate any underlying weaknesses and tendencies toward deterioration that existed in the city's housing market. Even as the city government grows increasingly alarmed at the prospect of becoming the world's biggest and most notorious slum landlord, and as it concomitantly improvises new increments of housing policy at ever-shorter intervals, there is no evidence that it has the problem under control, or that it has even accurately diagnosed it.

A further irony is that, media and public perceptions notwithstanding, the cancer of housing destruction exists in the midst of a city that is a great deal more vital than the central cities of most metropolitan areas of the nation. The city's economy may have declined from the peak it reached in 1969, but with 3.2 million jobs, it is still the

largest economic complex of the United States and probably the world. Its population may have declined, at least
partly because it has been repelled or displaced by the
ecology of housing destruction, but in absolute terms it is
still the largest municipal population of the country, and
its rate of decline is below that of most large American
central cities with fixed municipal boundaries. Even the
city's housing market is fundamentally vital. While hundreds of thousands of apartments fail to attract tenants,
however low their rents, in the city's viable neighborhoods
there prevails such a shortage of housing that housing
prices are skyrocketing (to the degree that rent regulation
permits). In the most fashionable parts of Manhattan the
price of housing exceeds that of any urban neighborhood
in the nation. Thus, the continuing housing destruction is
not the final spasm of a dying city, but a shocking and, in
this author's view, unnecessary anomaly.

That this anomaly has been tolerated for so long may be
partly due, as has been indicated, to the ineffectiveness of
ill-considered public policies. A large part of the blame,
however, can also be placed in the complacency of all the
partners directly involved in the marginal housing market,
and their belief that the status quo is preferable to any
substantial change in the system that might imperil some
of their vested interests.

The welfare bureaucracy has been so preoccupied with
the sheer immensity of its task of processing nearly 300,000
households every year through the system, that any change
that would increase its work load has been resisted. Its
principal concern is that every welfare family have a roof
over its head, without regard to the quality, permanence,
or cost of that roof. The welfare tenants themselves have
been so preoccupied with the challenge of understanding
the rules of the welfare game and wresting whatever mea-

ger benefits they can from it, that they have confined their complaints to ad hoc rent withholding rather than mounting any collective pressure.

The landlords, as an organized interest group, have been vociferous in their attacks on rent control, using the phenomenon of housing destruction as ammunition in their argument, but have been indifferent to other aspects of the ecology of destruction. Furthermore, even as owners ask us to commiserate in their growing poverty, an increasing body of new entrepreneurs are profitably exploiting conditions in the city's housing market, often by "selling short," as has been described in the previous chapter.

The courts, like the welfare bureaucracy, have been motivated principally by a determination to clear their calendars as expeditiously as possible. To the degree that they have exercised policy it has been one of simplistically scapegoating the landlords and turning a blind eye to tenant abuses.

The politicians in the city and in Albany have been too timid to confront the rent regulation issue head on because of its obvious and severe political implications in a city of tenants, and have contented themselves with some ill-advised tinkering with the system.

The city administration, while viewing the phenomenon with growing alarm, and after commissioning great numbers of studies, has been unwilling to confront the implications of changing the welfare system, the housing court, or rent regulation, and has often displayed the biases of these systems in any case. The only policies pursued have involved throwing more money, more regulations, and more people at the problem. This has meant using federal community development funds to manage abandoned buildings, hastening tax foreclosure, and trying to turn over abandoned buildings to tenants and community organizations. Nothing has been seriously contemplated to stop the process itself.

This is not to deny that a number of underlying trends have provided the conditions and the context that have nourished the process of housing destruction. The population of the city has declined, causing the demand for housing in many areas to become soft. The economy of the city has declined, eroding the fiscal base, impairing municipal services, and increasing unemployment among the city's poor. The percentage of minority families has increased, which has had a destabilizing effect on many neighborhoods that no public strategy could effectively counter.

What is being asserted here, then, is not that New York City can entirely escape the ravages of contemporary urban America; only that it can control circumstances sufficiently to assure that the physical environment and the quality of life generally, be no worse than in other cities or than the underlying circumstances would warrant.

What Is To Be Done

With 400,000 apartments already, or soon to be, lost to the forces of housing destruction clearly the process has gone quite far. Nevertheless with nearly 2 million rental units still remaining in the city as a whole and perhaps as many as 500,000 of them at risk, it is not too late to contemplate some changes in public policy to arrest the ecology of housing destruction. These changes will be controversial, unpopular and fraught with peril for any political figure who espouses them. Yet, unless they, or something like them, are implemented soon, the cancer will continue to spread to the point where it will drive a large proportion of the remaining middle income New York families from the city, and leave all of the Bronx, most of Brooklyn and large parts of Queens a wasteland.

The first policies that should be changed are those originating in the public sector institutions that interact most immediately to generate the ecology of housing destruction: the welfare system, rent regulation and the adjudicatory system. Each of these must change in significant ways as follows:

1. for all welfare households, rent specific housing allowances must be replaced with fungible flat grants that, in effect, enlarge the totally discretionary basic living allowance,
2. all forms of rent regulation must be eliminated for all apartments as they are vacated,
3. the adjudicatory system must be required to totally divorce considerations of housing maintenance from those of rent delinquency and insure that all proven rent delinquent tenants can be evicted.

Eliminating the Housing Allowance

Chapter III describes the way that New York State's practice of issuing to public assistance households separate and nonfungible housing allowances contributes to the process of housing destruction by:

a. fueling welfare tenant mobility, eventually creating a vacuum in housing demand in all areas that welfare families move through,
b. encouraging landlords to fill their buildings with welfare families, whatever their history of tenant responsibility,

c. condoning tenant irresponsibility with respect to rent payment and apartment maintenance.

In addition, the system violates recognized principles of income maintenance that prevail in the majority of the United States, by depriving welfare families of the right to spend their incomes as they see fit, including the right to decide on the importance to them of housing as an expenditure priority.

Virtually all of the negative effects on the housing market of the city's large (242,000 households) welfare population would be eliminated in one stroke if the non-fungible rent-specific shelter allowance were replaced with flat grants added to the basic living allottments which would allow welfare families to spend their entire income as they liked.

The present incentive to welfare tenant mobility arises because of several factors. As family size or circumstances change, the welfare family often becomes eligible for a larger shelter allowance that can only be realized if it moves into a more expensive apartment. More significantly, as long as a slack market exists beyond the area of welfare occupancy, ever better apartments become available whose rents fall within the shelter allowance ceilings; a temptation for all families, but especially for those whose present rents fall below the allowable maximums. Under these conditions, any welfare family would have to be foolish or lethargic not to take advantage of the possibilities offered by the shelter allowance system, particularly if it finds its neighborhood rapidly deteriorating around it.

The incentive for landlords to welcome even irresponsible welfare families into their buildings, in disregard of the long run impacts on other tenants or the buildings' asset value, arises from the warranty of rent paying ability implicit in the housing allowance, and the fact that the allowance guidelines may often exceed market rents.

Welfare families are tempted into irresponsible patterns of rent delinquency and mistreatment of their apartments because these practices can be profitable (e.g., spending the rent check, abusing the apartment to document code violations, inviting eviction to evade DSS moving constraints) and there are no effective sanctions imposed by the welfare system to deter them.

A system of flat grants, which to be fair should be pegged to the present shelter allowance maximums, would create an entirely contrary set of incentives. Welfare families would have an incentive to stay put, if not always in their present apartment, then at least in their present neighborhoods, because rents in outlying middle class areas beyond the frontier of welfare occupancy would undoubtedly be more expensive than their current ones. Those families who place a high priority on housing quality would, of course, be free to move and would manifest their interest in better housing by allocating a larger proportion of their budget to rent. Those who did so would be the most upwardly mobile and responsible families, ones who should have no destablizing effect on viable middle class neighborhoods. Most welfare families, however, would find it far more advantageous to stay in their present apartment, building or neighborhood. Vacancy rates in most areas of predominantly welfare occupancy are high enough, and the objective condition of the housing poor enough, that most apartments are presently overpriced, rent regulation notwithstanding. Those families that choose to stay put would be well positioned to bargain for a rent reduction, and would be entitled to pocket any ensuing savings, something that the present system does not permit. Any manifestation of apartment or building disrepair would create leverage in bargaining with the landlord, and would offer rent savings as a significant alternative to rent withholding (a practice that would be unavailing in any case if the other policy changes were effected). Even if rents were to rise to reflect increased heating and maintenance costs, they would be much lower in welfare families' present apartments than elsewhere.

With the elimination of the nonfungible and rent-specific shelter allowance, and above all the restricted two-party check, landlords would have to exercise the same care in selecting welfare tenants as they do for others. They would be encouraged to check any prospective tenant's history of rent payment and responsibility of tenure. To be sure, those landlords confronting a high vacancy rate or a badly maintained building could ill afford to be fussy. But at least in the better buildings at the fringe or beyond the zone of welfare occupancy, there would no longer be any reason to incur the risks of irresponsible welfare tenancy for short term gain because there would be no implicit or explicit rent-paying warranty behind any irresponsible tenant household. Even a reasonably high vacancy rate in a building occupied by responsible tenants (some of whom might be on welfare), would be preferable to an irresponsible welfare clientele with no shelter allowance system backing it up.

Under a flat grant system fewer welfare families would be irresponsible in the first place. Contrary to the prejudicial stereotypes entertained by the welfare bureaucracy as much as by the general public, welfare families are no more foolish or benighted than others. If the ability to secure a decent apartment depends on a satisfactory record of rent payment and apartment maintenance, most families will strive to maintain such a record. There would no longer be any advantages in engaging in a pattern of behavior that invites eviction because any move would have to be to a more expensive or, alternatively, less desirable apartment, and there would be the chastening risk of not being welcome anywhere. There would be no moving allowance, or reissued rent check, or new security deposit to ease the burden or cost of moving.

One can easily anticipate the various arguments or questions that will be offered to oppose a system of flat grants. Would it be legal? It would, if the New York State legislature passed legislation authorizing it. As has been indicated, flat grants for all living expenses, including rent, are already the norm in the majority of states; and the categorical segregation of income violates the prevailing philosophy of income maintenance.

Won't those welfare families who do not budget properly find themselves without housing altogether? At least this eventuality, it will be argued, is not possible under the present system. There are a number of responses that can be made to this line of reasoning. First, the likelihood of families with a stable source of income finding themselves without shelter at all, even in the event of personal irresponsibility, is exceedingly small as can be seen in the experience of the majority of states that already administer flat grants. Second, the assumption that welfare families, as a class apart from all others, need the special protection from personal irresponsibility afforded by the separate shelter allowance should be viewed as a gratuitous slur grounded in racial and class bigotry. The criterion for welfare eligibility is not irresponsibility, but an inability to join the labor force, either because of conflicting child rearing obligations or chronic unemployability. Third, it is only by allowing the normal sanctions of the marketplace to operate, that individuals and families are encouraged to be financially responsible. Finally, one could, as a companion measure to the implementation of a flat grant system, provide for the reservation of housing of last resort for families temporarily unable to secure housing on their own. Such housing could either be allocated out of the stock of public (New York City Housing Authority) housing or city-owned tax-foreclosed buildings, and should be available to all New York families that find themselves in such a position, regardless of their public assistance status.

Won't landlords abandon their buildings all the sooner if their poorest tenants no longer offered, at the minimum, the certainty or strong likelihood of a rent-paying ability set at levels unquestionably higher than those that would prevail if these tenants had to assume the rent burden out-of-pocket? This will be the argument of the landlords, and all those that subscribe to the rent gap theory. This view can be refuted by pointing out that, in terms of building cash flow, as the previous chapter indicated, the greatest threat to a building's viability is posed by low rent collection rates rather than low rents. Given the modest acquisition cost of most marginal property, if the entire potential rent roll were actually collectible, it would cover all carrying costs including upkeep, taxes and heat, and yield a fair return even if rents were very low. But in most marginal buildings today, only a fraction of the rent roll is collectible because of high, and rising, vacancy rates and flagrant rent delinquency. Apart from the adjudicatory system's contribution to rent delinquency, which will be addressed subsequently, both of these factors are exacerbated by the housing allowance system. Take away incentives for welfare tenants to keep on the move, and for landlords in threatened neighborhoods to welcome them, and vacancy rates will drop precipitously, even in the most marginal buildings. Remove the conditions that make welfare tenants complacent about the consequences of rent withholding and other irresponsible behavior, and the rate of rent delinquency will fall dramatically. The argument being offered here is that by encouraging low income families to stay put the elimination of the housing allowance would increase housing demand and tenant discipline in more marginal neighborhoods sufficiently to permit buildings to be profitable at low rents, and furthermore, would permit owners to maintain rents at levels high enough to insure profitability, assuming the constraints of rent regulation were removed.

Won't such a policy doom welfare families to living in slums? A response to this question involves both the observation that housing conditions for welfare families could hardly be worse than they are at present, where they are doomed not only to occupying slums, but ones that are being continually abandoned and destroyed out from under them, and the truism that, in the end, you get what you pay for. What the proponents of such an argument are really contending is that a consolidated flat grant will not be large enough to permit the average welfare family to satisfy its ordinary household expenditure requirements and have enough left over to pay for anything but the most unsatisfactory shelter. If that is indeed the case, the remedy lies in raising the level of welfare payments, not in earmarking a disproportionate share of a purportedly inadequate combined allotment for rent. Quite apart from the devastating effects that such a policy has had, it unmistakably asserts the New York State government's view that non-shelter expenditure priorities can be readily sacrificed, and that the welfare family cannot be trusted to determine the degree to which it should trade off housing amenity for the benefits of other goods and services.

It is probably true, given the size of the combined flat grant allotment (assuming shelter allowances folded in at their ceiling levels) for most welfare families, and given the preference that most welfare families will probably display for spending a large proportion of their income on non-housing items, that they will not have access to a very high quality housing stock. This does not mean, however, that they will be more poorly housed than they are today. Those members of the upwardly mobile minority who are willing to devote a large share of their income to housing will be able to find housing in stable neighborhoods that will not immediately collapse around them. For the rest, if the implementation of these recommendations brought a measure of stability to marginal neighborhoods, they might reap significant benefits from longer periods of building ownership, more responsible tenant behavior on the part of their neighbors, and greater freedom from the depredations of vandals and addicts preying on partially vacant structures.

Would this not simply invite a return to the ecology of the stable slum described earlier? Not necessarily. To the degree that today's poor have access, relatively speaking, to a much larger and more stable source of income than their predecessors, and to the degree that the private housing market is subject to much greater regulation and scrutiny than it was in the past, neighborhoods occupied by welfare families today could be far superior to the slums and ghettos of an earlier era. Under no circumstances would the elimination of the housing allowance create housing conditions more deleterious than prevail at the present time.

Ending Rent Regulation

The distortions created in the rental housing market by rent control and other forms of rent regulation are familiar to any serious student of housing policy, and their impact on housing in New York has been well documented in a number of studies. Chapter IV also indicated the ways in which rent regulation more specifically contributes to the ecology of housing destruction. Except for tenants and their advocates, there are very few people left in New York who will privately defend rent regulation. Nevertheless, no officials or politicians with large tenant constituencies have been willing to dismantle the system completely because of the obvious political repercussions. To mitigate the worst effects of rent control as they have interpreted them, they have implemented a series of changes in the system instead. These changes may have reduced the spread between regulated and market rents somewhat, but at the price of vastly increasing the complexity of the system. With these modifications, the actual distribution of allowable rents in the city's 1.3 million regulated apartments (two thirds of the market stock) is so idiosyncratic and bizarre that it not only defies the market, but defies considerations of logic and equity as well.

It is time to dismantle the system of rent regulation once and for all. This should include rent stabilization as well as rent control. In order to minimize the effects of deregulation on the present generation of tenants it is reasonable that apartments become deregulated only upon vacancy.

The argument has been advanced in Chapter IV that rent regulation has contributed significantly to the ecology of housing destruction by:

   a. depressing the asset value of the existing stock of apartment houses, making short term rental income exploitation followed by total disinvestment a viable economic strategy,
   b. depressing rent levels in stable neighborhoods to the extent that extensive penetration of such areas by poor (usually welfare) families has been encouraged,
   c. creating such a flat schedule of rent levels that apartments in changing neighborhoods seem overpriced to most nonwelfare families, relative to the

bargain (regulated) rentals available in much better areas,
d. holding the potential rental income in marginal
buildings hostage to often uneconomic maintenance requirements.

Beyond these manifestly destructive impacts, rent regulation has lowered the general quality of the housing stock
over three decades by reducing the economic attractiveness of new housing construction and the proper maintenance and rehabilitation of existing buildings. It has
distorted the pattern of demand both geographically and
in terms of the over consumption of large apartments by
small families. It is increasingly disadvantageous to the
tenant population itself by fueling the conversion of much
of the remaining viable rental housing to ownership (coop-
erative or condominium) tenure.

Perhaps as important as these direct housing market
effects, rent control and other forms of rent regulation
have hurt the city's housing stock by inculcating in the
city's tenant population the notion that it is entitled to
cheap housing, and cheap housing in fairly good condition,
at that. This orientation, in effect, demands that someone,
either private landlord or the government, subsidize virtually all housing in the city to the point that it would
allow the housing itself to be destroyed if these subsidies
could no longer be sustained. So pervasive has this attitude
become that it transcends the private sector and threatens
the publicly subsidized housing stock as well. One fourth
of the shallow city and state subsidized developments
(mainly Mitchell-Lama) are insolvent because their tenants (or tenant "owners" in the case of subsidized co-ops)
are outraged at the thought of paying rents and carrying
charges high enough to keep them viable. New York
State's experience with Co-op City, where tenants for five

years have resisted maintenance charge increases and mar-
shalled an enormous amount of political pressure in the
process, is illustrative.

The benefits that can be expected from an end to rent
regulation are not entirely symmetrical with the negative
effects enumerated above because many of these long
standing impacts have been thoroughly capitalized and
can no longer be undone, at least not quickly. Some effects, however, should be fairly immediate.

The most noticeable impact will be on the patterns of
housing demand. At the present time apartments are still
underpriced in the better neighborhoods of Manhattan
and Queens, and to a lesser extent Riverdale in the Bronx,
and the better sections of Brooklyn. Deregulation will permit rents in these areas to rise immediately, and will push
a significant increment of middle income demand into the
more marginal parts of the outer boroughs and stabilize
middle income demand already there. Because the highest
density parts of New York which contain some of the city's
most sophisticated and urbanized households are also the
most underpriced, it is highly unlikely that their excess
demand would be lured to the suburbs. Even if this new
increment of outer borough demand were to reside well
beyond the zones of destruction, it would stabilize all
neighborhoods, in a kind of reverse-musical chairs effect.

Another fairly immediate impact would be a rapid and
appreciable increase in the asset value of all desirable
apartment buildings in the city. In its ripple effects this
should eventually increase the asset value of all real property, including all but the worst buildings in marginal
neighborhoods. This should change the economic calculation of building ownership, reducing the economic attractiveness of short term rental income exploitation and
disinvestment, and increasing that of asset value conservation.

Many people will be surprised to find that with deregulation most rents in the city's less desirable areas will not rise appreciably, and in many instances they may even fall. Under unconstrained housing market conditions, tenants will pay for what they get in the way of housing amenity, and landlords of undesirable or poorly maintained buildings will have their rental income circumscribed by market rather than bureaucratic forces. Thus the citywide structure of rents should become considerably less flat, allowing for a fairly steep gradient that accurately reflects underlying demand considerations of location and apartment quality. This can only be salutary in a number of respects. Landlords will have the incentive, and potentially the income, to improve the maintenance and intrinsic quality of their buildings. Tenants will more accurately assess their need or desire for a particular location, a given amount of space, and a given level of amenity when these preferences must be manifested in paying a higher price. This will undoubtedly result in a greater degree of economic and class self-segregation.

But such self-segregation, which need not be accompanied by, or correlated with, racial segregation, should have a stabilizing effect on the city's housing in the aggregate. In fact, the families that have been most victimized by the naive assumption that long term economic and class integration is viable, have been upwardly mobile blacks and Hispanics who have not had the freedom of access to metropolitanwide housing vacancies that whites have had. It is moderate and middle income black and Hispanic families that, time and again, have striven to improve their housing environment by moving into ostensibly better parts of the city, only to see the forces of housing destruction overtake these neighborhoods with the invasion of poor, and often irresponsible, families.

Any proposal for deregulation will be met by fierce and broad based opposition, because by now the majority of New York City residents benefit from some form of rent regulation. Some of the arguments, other than an appeal to narrow self interest, will run as follows:

The middle class will no longer want, or be able to afford, to live in the city. This assumes that rent control and stabilization have served as important bribes to retain a middle income population which otherwise would have been repelled enough by crime, filth and a multitude of negative aspects of New York City life to leave. The fact that the middle class has been leaving the cheapest neighborhoods of the city in droves, while the more expensive (even under regulation) areas have prospered, clearly refutes this view. The kind of households that find city living attractive will stay even as rents rise, but may have to expand their geographical horizons somewhat to find affordable housing, which is all to the good. Those New Yorkers who have stayed only to take advantage of regulated rents are, by now, a distinct minority. Many of them have left the city already, most typically for a retirement community. Most of the rest are more concerned and alarmed by a rising tide of deterioration than the prospect of rent increases (however much they would protest them). In any case potential refugees from market rents would quickly find out that housing is much more expensive in the New York metropolitan area beyond the city's boundaries.

The poor will suffer. As has been indicated a number of times in a variety of contexts, the deregulation of rents will have the least noticeable impact on the buildings and neighborhoods occupied by the poor. The condition and location of this housing would warrant very little in the way of rent increases, and we may find that rent regulations are currently placing an arbitrary floor under rents that otherwise might actually fall. In any case, the benefits to poor families arising from the stabilization of their neighborhoods and a decline in the rate of abandonment would far outweigh the disadvantages of potentially modest rent increases. A variant of this argument would regret the loss of leverage inherent in a system which can gear rent increases to building maintenance. Yet, as has been argued earlier, the linkage between allowable rental income and building maintenance has only exacerbated the ecology of housing destruction.

Deregulation will create windfall profits for landlords. Even if this were true, it would be no reason to forego the beneficial effects on the housing market of deregulation. But most of the "windfall" would be absorbed in investments in building repairs and renovations that would be necessary to attract tenants in the kind of geographically expanded, competitive market that deregulation would create. The intense competition that presently exists among tenants for apartments in the city's better neighborhoods has made them much more tolerant of deficiencies in building or apartment condition than would be the case in a climate of market rents. In the city's marginal areas the "windfall" would be a wholesome incentive for owners to hold on to and maintain their properties.

In summary, then, it is hard to conceive of anything other than positive impacts arising from the elimination, upon vacancy, of rent control and rent stabilization for every regulated apartment in the city. All that is needed is an extreme exercise of political courage on the part of the city's and state's elected officials.

Reforming the Adjudicatory System

The great failing of the city's judiciary in housing cases, as has been indicated in Chapter V, is its unwillingness or inability to enforce the payment of rent. Some of this is due to the inefficiency of an overburdened system, but most of it resides in the legislatively sanctioned linkage of rent delinquency and code enforcement. The law creating the housing court, and the operative biases of the judicial system, make an owner's ability to collect rents from a delinquent tenant, or his right to evict him, conditional upon an ability to certify that his building and the tenant's apartment are free of code violations. Chapter V outlines the various ways in which this framework can be exploited by tenants and is dysfunctional in terms of sustaining the housing stock.

There is only one remedy. The adjudicatory system must completely disregard, in cases of nonpayment of rent, questions of building condition and code compliance. Tenant protection organizations, and the city on behalf of tenants, should be encouraged to sue for enforcement of the housing code or the tenant protective terms of leases. Under no circumstances should the courts sanction rent withholding as a remedy for complaints regarding building or apartment conditions. Nor should the courts make the eviction of rent delinquent tenants dependent on a finding of code compliance.

Implementing such a change of policy should not be very difficult. The housing court would be charged with adjudicating cases where landlords seek relief for nonpayment of rent or other purported tenant infractions solely on the basis of factors pertaining to the complaints. The court is already empowered to assess fines for documented code violations. More stringent sanctions for code violations and lease infractions than currently prevail could be legislated, including compensatory damages for tenants. Any adjudication of such cases must take full account, however, of the degree to which the landlord is actually responsible for the alleged deficiencies, their severity, and the economic impact, on rents especially, of correcting them.

Steps should also be taken to dispose of housing cases a

great deal more quickly by increasing the number of hearing officers, and devising more efficient procedures for ascertaining and documenting the facts. Landlords should also be encouraged to take a great deal more care in maintaining proper records regarding leases, rent receipts, expenditures for repairs, etc. The system should be designed to insure that landlords can obtain speedy relief (payment of back rent or eviction) from rent delinquency and tenants from unsatisfactory housing conditions.

Although somewhat less controversial than ending welfare housing allowances or rent regulation, this proposal will meet a great deal of opposition from those that feel the rent payment-code enforcement linkage is essential. The principal argument will be that rent withholding has proven to be the only effective sanction against unscrupulous landlords. As most housing cases are landlord initiated, and as few tenants have the resources, tenacity, or understanding of the law to press their complaints, it will be alleged that the kind of policy being espoused will make a dead letter of code enforcement. The three part rejoinder to this argument is that: (a) rent withholding and the rent payment-code enforcement linkage have not demonstrated their effectiveness in terms of improved code compliance, while they have threatened the economic viability of hundreds of thousands of apartments, (b) if code compliance is an important goal, it must be attacked directly by having the city devote adequate resources to it, and (c) if the other recommendations advanced here (elimination of separate housing allowances and rent regulation) were implemented, permitting landlords to collect their rents, they would have significant market incentives to maintain their buildings properly.

The hearing officer and others, when contemplating the possibility of sterner enforcement of rent payment, argue both that poor families cannot be thrown into the street, and that apart from a justification for rent withholding based on the inferior condition of their housing, they cannot afford to pay their rent. These views might carry some weight if a policy of leniency toward rent delinquent tenants permitted them to enjoy, in perpetuity, occupancy of their free (and perhaps newly repaired) apartments. But experience has shown that a policy that reduces rental income results in abandonment, eventually throwing not only the offending tenants, but all of their neighbors "into the street" as well.

Again, it must be reiterated that it cannot be public policy to thrust the economic burden of housing an impoverished population, dependent on implicitly inadequate income maintenance allowances, on an unsubsidized private housing sector. In the unlikely event that some families would really be unable to find housing anywhere, the public, not private, sector must be the houser of last resort. If many New Yorkers are too poor, even with public assistance, to afford to pay their rent, then their welfare allotments should be raised. In the end nothing that the judiciary does can compel the private landlord to provide decent shelter without adequate compensation.

Other Policies

In addition to the foregoing changes related specifically to the ecology of housing destruction, several other policy initiatives must be undertaken.

For the replacement of welfare housing allowances with flat grants, and the ending of rent control to have the maximum beneficial effect on the existing housing stock, there must be some restriction of the volume and location of new housing. The way in which the rapid enlargement of the housing stock in the 1960's, much of it built with public subsidies, and unjustified by a concomitant increase in population, contributed to the epidemic of housing detruction was discussed in Chapter II. Obviously there must be some replenishment and revitalization of the housing stock if the quality of housing, in the aggregate, is to improve. This must be accomplished in a way which is not harmful to existing neighborhoods. Several principles consistent with this objective can be identified.

First, as much as possible, the market for new development should be satisfied in the rehabilitation of apartments in the better buildings of the existing stock.

Second, new development, whether in totally new construction or rehabilitation, should be directed away from the areas of very intense development pressure such as the fashionable parts of Manhattan and Queens, to areas that, while possessing good potential for long range viability, have been by-passed or ignored because of the increasing locational selectiveness of the development market. This selectiveness is itself a product of, and reaction to, the ecology of housing destruction; an unwillingness, in a very unstable housing situation, to gamble on anything but the sure thing. Understandable as it might be, this kind of geographic selectivity, outside of the zones of destruction, should not be encouraged or facilitated.

Third, the volume of subsidized new construction should be fairly strictly limited to what realistically can be absorbed in a city with a declining population without draining the still desirable existing buildings and neighborhoods of their tenants.

Property tax assessment and abatement is another policy area where new initiatives could profitably support the remaining housing stock and help to retard the process of housing destruction. Most properties in marginal and deteriorating neighborhoods of the city are overassessed. If the owners of these properties have the patience and tenacity, they can eventually have their assessments lowered to realistic levels. Most, however, will probably relinquish ownership before even initiating, let alone exhausting, the long assessment appeals process. Therefore, a policy initiative to reduce assessments in all fragile areas of the city, before tax delinquency and abandonment take place, would be very desirable. Beyond this step in the direction of simple equity, the city should seriously consider granting blanket tax abatements for classes of structures (determined according to criteria which reflect present building condition, degree of owner responsibility, etc.) in specified parts of the city that would be deemed neighborhood conservation areas. High property taxes are not the principal element in housing abandonment and destruction, but they constitute an important marginal factor for many buildings. In any case, the lighter the tax burden, the less likely that tax delinquency and foreclosure will permanently seal their fate.

Making the foregoing policy recommendations is not to imply that there has been a lack of inventiveness on the part of the city's policy establishments in proposing remedies to deal with the various aspects of New York's crisis of housing deterioration and abandonment, the city's poor record of success notwithstanding. Unfortunately, some of these remedies are misdirected in their diagnosis of the problem; others are too limited in scope, and some of the best ideas have never been implemented. Two notions, however, stand out in terms of both their popularity and their wrongheadedness.

One is the idea of placing all, or a large proportion of welfare families on restricted (two-party) checks.[1] This is very popular with landlords, most city officials, and a number of academic housing economists, because it is supposed to increase landlords' rental income; it is very unpopular with HEW and welfare rights groups because it reduces tenant discretion.[2] The concept is grounded in the same principle that has animated many of the recommendations made earlier in this chapter: that marginal rental properties are much more apt to be economically viable if their rents are fully collectible. But, as discussed at length in Chapter III, the restricted check approach to implementing that principle exacerbates the vacancy-creating syndrome of excessive welfare tenant mobility which is one of the cornerstones of the ecology of housing destruction.

The other notion is the proposal to turn over as many tax-foreclosed properties as possible to tenant cooperatives or community-based organizations. This proposal assumes that the wicked and exploitative landlord would be replaced with tenants and dedicated members of the community, creating a class of owner-managers who would have a stake in the survival of the property. Also, by forgoing taxes and offering rehabilitation subsidies in the bargain, these structures' economic viability would be assured. Limited experience to date would seem to refute these optimistic assumptions. Existing community or tenant-managed buildings are plagued by the same problems of high vacancy rates and rent delinquency as all others. Nor has the job of finding and training owner/managers been very easy or successful. Beyond these probably fatal flaws in this proposal, the city could never muster the bureaucratic energy to solve the problems of 246,000 tax foreclosed structures in such a building-by-building procedure.

What these and most other ideas being bandied about share in common, and where they depart most substantially from our recommendations, is in their reliance on ever more detailed and fussy intervention in New York City's housing market on the part of one or another agency of government. One does not have to be an advocate of laissez-faire, nor an ideological conservative, to remark that when it comes to housing in New York City, the public sector has done quite enough already. Up to now every new increment of public intervention has made things worse. There have been so many unsuccessful twists and turns along the path of well-intentioned tinkering that perhaps it is time to test the possibility that the generally reasonable incentives and discentives of an unconstrained market might do a better job of allocating and conserving the housing stock.

Conclusion

There is no question that, on balance, the post war decades have not dealt much more kindly with New York City than they have with other older central cities of the United States. New York has been no exception to the pattern of declining economies, departing middle class white families, inflows of poor minority families, rising rates of crime and other social pathologies, increasing financial strain, and increasing rates of neighborhood deterioration persisting in the face of statistically documented improvements in the condition of individual dwelling units.

The easily observable objective conditions in New York that have motivated this study and its insistence that this city's problems transcended the kinds of exogeneous factors just alluded to are:

a. The rate of housing destruction has far exceeded the rate of population loss, and may have actually precipitated some population loss. Since 1965 the city has lost no more than 150,000 households, while it has lost easily 300,000 dwelling units.

b. The geographical and numerical extent of housing destruction and neighborhood deterioration far exceeds the extent of poverty and social pathology prevailing among the city's residents. Approximately 13.3 percent of the city's population is comprised of members of desperately poor families, most of them on welfare, yet something like 25 percent of the city's dwelling units and perhaps as much as one third of its developed land area is already, or about to be, embraced by the waves of devastation.

c. Most of the objective indicators of urban vitality are actually more favorable for New York than they are for other central cities not nearly so ravaged. The city still has more jobs, more people, and more elements of intrinsic desirability than any other in the nation, as is manifested, among other ways, in an incredibly tight and expensive housing market in Manhattan and many parts of the other boroughs.

Having launched the study on the basis of these observations, after tracing and documenting the interlocking impacts of various public and private policies that are relatively unique to this city, at least in combination, we remain convinced that the ecology of housing destruction is, indeed, largely an artifact of public policy and, thus, will require a redirection of public policy to reverse, including a significant reduction in the scope of direct public intervention.

NOTES

1. N.Y.S. Department of Social Services, "A Demonstration in the Use of Two-Party Rent Checks." Application to U.S. HEW *op. cit.*
2. Henry A. Freedman, Timothy J. Casey, Memorandum to U.S. HEW, "Urging Disapproval of Proposed New York (AFDC Two-Party Rent Check) Project," Downtown Welfare Advocate Center, 15 March 1979.

BIBLIOGRAPHY

A. General Policy and Data

1. Bales, Carter F.; and Puri, Anupam P. *A Housing Agenda for New York City.* McKinsey and Company, 1974.
2. Lowry, Ira S.; DeSalvo, Joseph S.; and Woodfill, Barbara M. *Rental Housing in New York, The Demand for Shelter.* The New York City Rand Institute, June 1971.
3. Lowry, Ira S. *Rental Housing in New York City, Confronting the Crisis.* The New York City Rand Institute, February 1970.
4. New York City Department of City Planning. *Planning for Housing in New York City,* 22 August 1977.
5. New York City Department of City Planning. *New Dwelling Units Completed 1921-1972,* December 1973.

144

6. New York City Housing and Development Administration. *The Rental Housing Situation in New York City 1975*, January 1976.
7. New York State Division of Housing and Community Renewal. *Construction Activity in New York State*, January 1978.
8. Quigley, John M. "Housing Policy Priorities in the New York Region." *New York Affairs*, September 1978.
9. Real Estate Research Corporation, *A Policy Review of Rental Housing in New York City*, April 1975.
10. "Moderate Rehabilitation Projects—Evaluation of SHF's Recent Experiences," Settlement Housing Fund, 1978.
11. Sternlieb, George (with James W. Hughes). *Housing and People in New York City*, January 1973.
12. Sternlieb, Roistacher and Hughes, *Tax Subsidies and Housing Investment*, Center for Urban Policy Research, 1976.
13. Sternlieb, George and Hughes, James W. *Housing and Economic Reality: New York City 1976*, Center for Urban Policy Research, 1976.
14. Sternlieb, George and Hughes, James W. "*New York City 1985.*" Center for Urban Policy Research, 1978.
15. Tobier, Emanuel. *Aspects of the New York City Property Market*. Citizens Housing and Planning Council of New York, December 1975.
16. U.S. Department of Commerce, Bureau of the Census. *Annual Housing Survey: 1976, New York, N.Y. SMSA*. September 1978.
17. U.S. Department of Commerce, Bureau of the Census. *New York City Housing and Vacancy Survey*, 1978.

B. *Housing Abandonment and Neighborhood Deterioration*

1. Kristof, Frank S. "Housing Abandonment in New York City." *Conference on Housing, Georgia State University,* 8 May 1978.
2. Leven, Charles L. et. al., *Neighborhood Change, Lessons in the Dynamics of Urban Decay,* Praeger, 1976.
3. McGaughey, Lawrence H. *"New York City in Rem Property Sales Study."* New York Coalition Housing Rehabilitation Task Force, August 1975.
4. New York City Planning Commission. "Report on the Fifth Year Community Development Plan and Program, In Rem Housing Section," April 1979,
5. New York City Finance Administration. "1977-78 Real Estate Statistics on Property Tax Arrears," 21 March 1978.
6. Sternlieb, George, and Burchell, Robert W. *Residential Abandonment: The Tenement Landlord Revisited.* Center for Urban Policy Research, 1973.
7. Sternleib, George. "A Brief Statement on the Nature and Magnitude of the Abandonment Problem." Center for Urban Policy Research, 10 December 1978.
8. Women's City Club of New York. *With Love and Affection: A Study of Building Abandonment,* 1977.

C. *Publicly Assisted Housing*

1. Muchnick, David M. *Financial Realities in Publicly Assisted Housing* (A report on Mitchell—Lama and Federally Insured Housing Developments in New York). Citizens Housing and Planning Council of New York, 1977.
2. New York City Department of City Planning. *Public*

and Publicly-Aided Housing, 1927-1973, September 1974.

3. New York City Housing and Development Administration. *Summary of Government Housing Activity in New York City,* 1973.
4. New York City Housing and Redevelopment Administration. *Directory of Publicly-Aided Housing Developments,* 1971.
5. New York City Mayor's Policy Committee. *Housing Development and Rehabilitation in New York City,* November 1974.
6. New York State Division of Housing and Community Renewal. *Analysis of Mitchell-Lama Company Financial Operations,* February 1977.
7. New York State Division of Housing and Community Renewal. *Statistical Summary of (Publicly Assisted Housing) Programs,* 31 March 1977.
8. New York State Office of the State Comptroller, Division of Audits and Accounts. *Report on the Viability of Housing Projects Financed by the New York State Housing Finance Agency,* 1976.

D. Welfare Housing

1. Freedman, Henry A., and Casey, Timothy J. Memorandum to U.S. HEW "Urging Disapproval of Proposed New York (AFDC Two-Party Rent Check) Project." Downtown Welfare Advocate Center, 15 March 1979.
2. Lowry, Ira S.; Gueron, Judith M.; and Eisenstadt, Karen M. *Welfare Housing in New York City.* The New York City Rand Institute, November 1972.
3. New York City Department of City Planning, "People on Public Assistance by Census Tract," 1978.

4. New York City Department of Social Services. *Procedures Manual, H-1 Housing Section*, February 15, 1978.

5. New York City Human Resources Administration, Office of Research and Program Evaluation. *Quarterly Rent Reports, 1970-1978*.

6. New York State Department of Audit and Control, Office of Welfare Inspector General, *An Examination of Rental Payments Made to Private Landlords by New York City Public Assistance Recipients*, February 1, 1977.

7. New York State Department of Social Services, Application to U.S. HEW for "A Demonstration in the Use of AFDC Two-Party Rent Checks to Encourage Housing Repairs and to Aid Neighborhood Stabilization," December 13, 1978, and response to U.S. HEW Commissioner B.L. VanLare by New York State Commissioner B.B. Blum, January 25, 1979.

8. Sternlieb, George S. (with Bernard P. Indik). *The Ecology of Welfare*. Transaction Books, New Brunswick, N.J., 1973.

9. U.S. Department of Health, Education and Welfare, Social Security Administration. *Characteristics of State Plans for Aid to Families with Dependent Children*, 1977.

E. Rent Regulation

1. Briggs, B. Bruce. "Rent Control Must Go." *New York Times Magazine*, 8 April 1976.

2. Franklin, J. James, and Lett, Monica R. (for the Rent Stabilization Association of the New York City), *The Economics of Rental Housing New York City, The Effects of Rent Stabilization*, 22 May 1976.

3. Kristof, Frank S. "Rent Control Within the Rental Housing Parameters of 1975," The American Real Estate and Urban Econmics Association Journal, Vol. 3, No. 3, Winter, 1975, pp. 47-60.

4. Kristof, Frank S. *The Effects of Rent Control and Rent Stabilization in New York City.* New York City Temporary Commission on City Finances, June 1977.

5. New York City Conciliation and Appeals Board, *Year's End Report, January 1, 1976-December 31, 1976.*

6. New York City Housing and Development Administration, *Analysis of MBR and Vacancy Decontrol Impact on Rent Levels and Building Maintenance,* 12 January, 1973.

7. New York Telephone, Environmental Analysis Division, Corporate Planning Department. *Rent Control at the Grassroots,* 5 March 1976.

8. Rent Stabilization Association of New York. *A Reference Source to the Rent Stabilization Code of 1969.*

9. Rent Stabilization Association of New York, *Final Submission and Comments of the Rent Stabilization Association to the Rent Guidelines Board,* 15 March 1979.

10. Sharov, Itzhak. *Vacancy Decontrol.* Community Housing Improvement Program, 6 February 1974.

11. Teplin, Albert M. "The Scope of Residential Rent Control Laws: A Preliminary Study," unpublished paper, January 1977.

F. Adjudicatory System and Code Enforcement

1. New York Ctiy Housing and Development Administration. *HDA Housing Court Operations,* 1973.

2. New York City Housing and Development Admin-

istration. *Housing Maintenance Code and Violation Order Numbers,* March 1973.

3. New York City Office of the Comptroller. *Performance Analysis of the City Housing Court,* 7 January 1977.

INDEX